the Cactus Sandwich

and other Tall Tales of the Southwest

by Don Dedera
Illustrations by Bill Ahrendt
Foreword by C. L. Sonnichsen

NORTHLAND PRESS FLAGSTAFF, ARIZONA

*To F.V. (Bud) Brown,
dean of southwestern mule champions,
and to his lifelong companion, Isabelle,
who is perhaps the best endurance horsewoman
Arizona has ever known, this book is
affectionately dedicated.*

Contents

The Professional Prevaricator— Artist at Work

umor specialists (every college has at least one) should let this book alone. It is meant to be enjoyed for its own sake. To look for origins of these tales in Yugoslavia or Texas or other foreign lands would certainly be superfluous. A few readers, however, are going to curl the lip and look down the nose at these inventions even as they laugh at them, and such people need to be reasoned with. They need to learn that these are not just "thigh-slapping utterances" (Dedera's phrase)—that they deal with the sorrows of mankind and involve the search for truth. These skeptics can enjoy the stories and perceive these truths at the same time.

Laughter itself, we all need to remember, is a godsend to human beings and could have replaced Hope at the bottom of Pandora's box. It offers relief from monotony and boredom and can make the unbearable endurable. When we are too hot or too cold or too hungry or too scared to go on with the Cosmic Farce, we learn to laugh at it, thereby saving our souls and our reason.

Here is where the search for truth comes in. Exaggeration makes truth easier to grasp. When the soldier dies at Yuma, goes to hell, and sends back for his blankets (Dedera says it was his overcoat), we understand how hot it gets at Yuma. Stories about sandstorms, wild creatures, the landscape, the Grand Canyon, imaginary animals—all conceal some truth about life and land in Arizona.

But there is more to it than that. The storytellers are just as important to us as the stories. The personalities of the narrators are an indispensable part of the total effect. Ever since the days of the Greeks and Romans, people have enjoyed oddballs—individualists who refuse to be like other people. They think and talk as they please and break the rules when they feel like it. We enjoy them because they flout the conventions the rest of us have to live by. They can lie big if they want to.

Besides, they lie with masterly skill and are champions in their own line as much as Ben Hogan and Jack Dempsey were in theirs. People are fascinated by supreme skill in anything and these are masterly liars.

In this case the skills are a cut above muscular coordination. They involve the intellect and come close to poetry. Great liars use the poet's tool—the imagination.

Remember what the imagination does. It presents images—brings pictures to the eye and sounds to the ear. It makes thought visible. How hot is it in the Arizona desert? Well, consider the stick lizards. When they cross the Centennial Wash, they "carry sticks in their mouths, and when they can no longer bear the burning sand, they jab the sticks into the ground and shinny up them to cool their feet." Now you know how hot it is because you see it. That is how imagery works. Compare Shelley's inscription on the ruined statue of the great Ozymandias: "Look on my works, ye mighty, and despair."

Arizona provoked hyperbole, especially where life was difficult. The country people, says Dedera, were "the product of a lifeway manifestly lonesome, dangerous, introspective, outdoor, workworn, shy, unintellectual, and male." Their existence, he adds, "was an outrageous gamble, and why not recreation?" Recreation, of course, included outrageous tale-telling.

In short, Arizona's professional prevaricators live in a country that can't be described in ordinary terms, where life is beyond conventional expression, where natives have to turn to something like poetry to make things clear. Their lies are creative and imaginative, and the fact that they are funny is the frosting on the cake.

Jim Griffith is getting close to this idea when he risks the statement that "stories are beautiful, and that human-made beauty is enormously important in any form." I would modify Jim's statement to say that human achievement in any form is enormously important, sometimes beautiful, always interesting, and that the stories of these professional prevaricators are indeed an extraordinary human achievement.

Hamlin Garland sums it up. He could have been talking about Charles Dickens when he praised John Hance, the Homeric Liar of the Grand Canyon, as a "powerful and astonishing fictionist . . . one of the most dramatic and picturesque natural raconteurs I have ever met." The sentence that follows, however, leaves Dickens in England and locates the subject firmly in Arizona. Hance's profanity, says Garland, "blazes out like some unusual fireworks and illuminates his story for yards around." Burdened by his taboos and reticencies, Dickens would not have played in Hance's league. Arizona liars have created a world of their own.

C. L. Sonnichsen
Tucson

Words That Won
the West

I t may be overstating the obvious, but this little book is not intended as a serious work. The author, as a daily newspaper
columnist over a fifteen-year stint, first fell from grace by serving as a public message center for incorrigible and persistent
liars. So innocently begun, the association led to smallish ex-
tensions of white fibs, then to outright lying, and finally to the
most serious class of untruthfulness—telling lies about lies. Another
decade as a free-lance writer refined and elaborated the weakness.
Association with hard-bitten, professional prevaricators—mostly
lawyers—completed the ruin.

My only chance for leniency may rest in my restricted arena of
lying. I've generally limited my sins to Arizona and adjacent parts of
the American Southwest . . . the last half of the twentieth century and
attached portions of the past and present . . . and civilized com-
munities plus big towns such as Phoenix and mere holes in the
ground like Grand Canyon. And to this weak defense I might add
the bleat of so many confessors awaiting sentence: "I never meant to
do it."

Some folks DO take falsehood seriously. Nor is all of this
harmless fun. The first organized exploration of the Southwest by

1

Europeans held faith in the tall tales of Estevan as certified by Fray Marcos de Niza. Twenty years ago, no less an authority than Dr. Ray Allen Billington (Harmsworth Professor of American History at Oxford, to become director of the Bancroft Library) advanced a theory that whoppers and windies in a public relations effect amounted to the "words that won the West." As an example: scientific assays of western gold ore often went unbelieved, but taken as gospel was the story of a prospector who found an 849-pound nugget, refused to give up the unmovable, and sat down on it and offered $27,000 for a plate of pork and beans. Today, Dr. Billington's ideas about exaggeration as a human motivator are expanded upon by Dr. James (Big Jim) Griffith, director of the Southwest Folklore Center at the University of Arizona, and by Professor Don L.F. Nilsen, chair, Western Humor and Irony Membership, at Arizona State University. Both of these worthies rattle on endlessly about schools of sand trout in the dry Santa Cruz River, and cowboy coffee so strong "it will slip the hoof off a boar hog." Griffith and Nilsen and other scholars discern social import in the works of Mark Twain, John A. Lomax, Badger Clark, John Hance, Lewis Nordyke, Frank M. King, Ramon F. Adams, Mody Boatright, Neil M. Clark, J. Frank Dobie, Oren Arnold, Stan Hoig, Charlie Pickrell, and C.L. Sonnichsen, all extraordinary liars or collectors of lies when they chose to be.

Within better tall tales, of course, lurks a measure of truth. Arizona truly embraces the superlative called Grand Canyon of the Colorado. Naturally enough, the pioneer guide Captain John Hance claimed that it was dug by a Scot who lost a nickel, and where he piled the dirt became the 12,670-foot San Francisco Peaks. Hance, who maybe did and maybe didn't lose an index finger in the Civil War, informed tourists that he had rubbed the digit short by pointing out the scenery. Hance also told how he survived a fall, horseback, into the mile-deep canyon. "When the horse and I were three feet from the bottom, I hauled back on the reins and yelled, 'Whoa!'" An Arizonan who stands in the front rank of American storytellers is Dick Wick Hall, he of the Laughing Gas Service Station made famous in the *Saturday Evening Post*.

It has been my privilege and pleasure to trade forgeries with accomplished Arizona folklorists. Oren Arnold was a close friend who earned more fees as a free-lance writer revising the myth of the Lost Dutchman gold mine than he made with any verifiable nonfiction article of his long and illustrious career. Charles U. Pickrell, Milo Wiltbank, John Myers Myers, Gussie Thomas Smith, Roscoe Willson, Reverend Charles Franklin Parker, Bob Capps, Ray Duus, Bill Bass, Ed Peplow, Kearney Egerton, Reg Manning, Herbert A. Leggett, Dave Hicks, Julius Festner, Tom Tarbox, and Don Schellie were in some degree or another co-conspirators; and at this writing, still-active partners-in-crime include Maggie Wilson, James E. Cook, Marguerite Noble, F.V. (Bud) Brown, Dr. Frank Honsik, Bob Hirsch, C.L. Sonnichsen, Charlie Niehuis, Katie Lee, Joe Beeler, Marshall Trimble, Dennis R. Freeman, Charlie Pine, Bill Sizer, Joe Bethancourt, Rex Allen Sr., Jim Spero, Paul Dean, Sam Lowe, and Budge Ruffner. The outrageously misleading images created by artist Bill Ahrendt for this book manifest a genius in pettifoggery.

Giving proper credit to originators of folktales is generally impossible. Arizona is youngest of the mainland states, and tall tales accompanied the several waves of migration. Old stories acquired new settings and characters. It is not at all unusual for a folklorist belatedly to determine that an Arizona Al plot once worked a miracle for Davey Crockett. We know that Paul Bunyan was born in the woods of Maine where as a babe "he rolled around so much in his sleep he knocked down four square miles of standin' timber." That tale also is retold in Arizona logging camps harvesting some of the state's two billion board feet of pine. Pecos Bill, raised by coyotes, taught them to howl. And how Bill's brown pals now yowl in Arizona! Mike Fink, Jim Bridger, Big Foot Wallace, Febold Feboldson, Joe Magarac, Gib Morgan, John Henry, and Johnny Appleseed prosper reincarnate amongst the cactus and canyons of Arizona. In all humility, I discovered recently that the winning entry in a statewide tall-tale contest, which I oversaw in 1967, was somewhat rewritten to win the Scottsdale, Arizona, folklore competition in 1975. Humility, I say, because also only recently I found a written version two hundred years old!

All that said, from the perspective of Arizona, particular debts are owed to trailblazing by B.A. Botkin, editor of *A Treasury of American Folklore*; Mody Boatright, prolific collector of southwestern folktale; and J. Frank Dobie, preeminent cross-pollinator of Texas/Arizona folk wisdom. Some of their classics, together with a prejudiced bibliography, are recommended in a list of selected readings at the back of this book.

What is truth? Pilate asked. Truth is what you can make people believe, the cynic ever has responded. But in Arizona, truth is an especially difficult product to manage. Truth by itself boggles. It is provable geometrically that the length of Arizona approximates the distance from Washington, D.C., to Toledo, Ohio. Arizona was explored by Europeans eighty years before Plymouth Rock. By the year A.D. 1000, a now-vanished people were irrigating fifty thousand acres of farms with five hundred miles of canals in Arizona's Salt River Valley. The Hopi Indian village of Oraibi, Arizona, may be the oldest continuously occupied town in America. Living specimens of the creosote bush of Arizona and neighboring deserts are as old as ten thousand years—in clone form the oldest life on earth. The bowl called Meteor Crater in northern Arizona was created in an instant fifty thousand years ago; today it could seat three million football fans. From one rainfall, a giant saguaro cactus may drink a ton of water. Arizona's largest county is half again as large as Maryland. The American cattle industry was begun in Arizona. Among startling placenames in Arizona are a canyon, Wickytywiz; a mine, Total Wreck; a mountain, Wrong; a rapid, Sockdolager; and a town, Why. Not unusual: in the same day's weather report, Yuma, Arizona, will be the warmest spot in the nation, and Alpine, Arizona, the coldest. If New York City were populated as sparsely as the vast stretch of Arizona north of Grand Canyon, only sixteen people would occupy all those skyscrapers of Manhattan. So much for the boring truth.

Moonshine makes it believable. In one of the postulations advanced two decades ago by Dr. Billington, "Exaggeration, carried to the point of fantasy, has wide appeal if presented with tongue-in-cheek humor. Not even the most gullible could believe that Oregon hogs ran about already cooked, or that Californians had to leave their healthy climate to die, or that a miner could sit for sixty-seven days on an 849-pound nugget and offer fantastic sums for pork and beans. Yet these were the tall tales that were reprinted everywhere, and remembered. They did as much to advertise the West, and with less effort by their originators, than the most unromantically accurate statements."

...But How Hot Did It Get?

here U.S. Route 89 crosses the Hassayampa River at Wickenburg, Arizona, observant motorists are startled by a little sign cautioning NO FISHING FROM BRIDGE. Startled they are because nearly always the river is bone dry. Enterprising burghers know what they are about. Tourists slam to a halt and investigate a roadside shrine promising that one cool sip at a bubbler of Hassayampa well water will convert the drinker to a hopeless liar.

Bemused visitors tarry long enough to discover that Wickenburg also offers clean rooms and good grub downtown, genuine western hospitality, casual shopping, and dude ranch luxury not far outside town. Travelers stay over a few days, spend more than a few dollars, and depart, never to tell the truth again. And the good folks of Wickenburg annually freshen the paint on their NO FISHING sign.

Within Wickenburg's gentle deceit prospers an Arizona and far southwestern tradition: the telling of tall tales. The exercise is the local contribution toward exaggeration characteristic of the American West. The leg of the tenderfoot is tugged. But the more worthy whoppers bolster a regional truism—that Arizona, for example, can be hot and dry.

How dry? How hot?

My own favorite in four decades of collecting southwestern folktales:

The morning after a fierce dust storm a rancher inspected his spread in the dunes country near Yuma, Arizona. He spied a fancy cowboy hat lying by the side of the road. Assuming a fortunate windfall, he picked up the sombrero only to reveal a pale bald scalp—that of a cowboy, who explained he had been caught in the storm the night before.

"Wait," said the Samaritan. "I'll fetch a shovel from the truck and dig you out."

"Better go back to town and bring a tractor," suggested the cowboy. "I'm a-sittin' on my horse!"

The story for me ranks as a classic because the setting is unmistakably regional, the weather is grim but grand, the resident hero prevails, and tall as the story may loom, it's mercifully short. No active practitioner of the art of tale-telling excels one Lester (Budge) Ruffner, fourth generation Arizonan, book critic, author, and raconteur of the old territorial capital of Prescott. Budge's own prizewinner:

"Seems one day that this Mexican cowman was attempting to impress Charles White of the Arizona Bank. The Mexican said his ranch was wonderful...that all it lacked was water."

"White replied, 'That's all *Hell* needs is water!' "

One August at Gila Bend, swears Harquahala rancher William Howard O'Brien, the sun burned an angry red brand across the high blue sky. Took a week to heal. The trails dried up to salt.

But that wasn't how hot it got.

Bob Robles notes that before statehood a cavalryman died of sunstroke at Fort Yuma, went to Hell, and telegraphed back for his overcoat. He was the one who had shouted from the crematorium, "Shut that door! I can't stand a draft!" When they posted the death certificate they had to staple the stamp. They primed the mourners at the funeral. The Holy Water was only thirteen percent moisture, and was wet only on one side. The chaplain took advantage of the service to complain to the Lord that the winters at Yuma were so gorgeous, Heaven was unappealing by comparison, and the summers were so horrible, Hell held no terror.

It was General Phil Sheridan who informed Congress, "We fought one war with Mexico to win Arizona. We ought to fight another to make her take it back." Kit Carson grumped, "Not even a wolf can make a living there." Somewhere Ted O'Malley read that in the early days in Tucson the only way to keep cool was to stand around a blazing lumber yard. A newcomer, on sighting a roiling brown cloud racing across the desert, inquired, "A dust storm?" "Nope," said a native. "The river's up." That was the year the peanuts were dug up roasted and salted. The rocks turned black. Randy Irvine said it got so hot, there was nothing to do but pull off your skin and sit around in your bones.

Isabelle Brown recalls that her pioneer grandaddy, Vi (for Revilo, or Oliver spelled backwards) Fuller, once vowed, "Why, it got so hot and dry, when we bought an old sow, we had to soak her in a horse trough for three days before she'd hold swill."

Yet it does get hotter. Dana Burden tells about the Centennial Wash stick lizards, which down through the blazing eons have evolved a system for traveling across the blistering desert. They carry sticks in their mouths, and when they no longer can bear the searing sand, they jab the sticks into the ground and shinny up the sticks to cool their feet.

And hotter. Salome is the home of the frog that carries a canteen of water for moistening the moss on its back. According to Salome's late humorist, Dick Wick Hall, sometimes in the desert the days are so hot that in races of life-and-death, the coyotes and jackrabbits agree to walk.

"Too hot to quarrel," Hall wrote one summer. "So the Ladies Aid Society didn't meet this week."

Hall also had the last word on desert: "I got a letter from a man yesterday wanting to know Why it was so Dry on the Desert, so I wrote and told him it wouldn't be a Desert if it Wasn't, which was Why it Was."

For his desert vegetables Hall tapped a logical source of moisture: "We plant onions in between the potatoes and then Scratch the onions to make the potato Eyes water enough to irrigate the rest of the garden."

Dry? Listen to Will Rogers when he followed President Calvin Coolidge to the rostrum at the dedication of Coolidge Dam in 1926. The Gila River for years had shrunk to a trickle. Said Will, "If that was my lake, I'd mow it."

Hot? Until his own untimely demise, cartoonist Kearney Egerton related how an easterner wearing a blue serge suit boarded the Southern Pacific in Benson one late July day, and when the train pulled into Tucson, only the suit stepped off the train. The easterner had evaporated.

One torrid summer, when the sun stood straight overhead like a burnished plaque, a half-dozen dead mesquite stumps crawled out of their holes to a spot of shade. That was the same year, according to newsman C.R. (Dick) Waters, that a joshua tree hiked into Bullhead City and impersonated a fire plug. A painted lady from Laughlin put four quarters in it thinking it was a shaggy slot machine. When Charlie Waters was old enough to talk, his first words were, "Dad, when was the last time it rained in Blythe?" And Dad (Dick) responded honestly, "Not in my time here, son." Charlie was twelve years old before he saw rain, on a vacation to Hawaii. Dick used to maintain that Mohave County was the only land in America where you had to climb for water and dig for wood. A cloud drifting in from San Francisco one summer almost evaporated on the desert...got a transfusion from Lake Mead...and limped on into Wickiup. Cattle dried up so small they could hide out in the henhouse.

But that was not a record heat. Douglas-born Jack Yelverton tells about a Chiricahua rancher who rode into town one early September to surrender to the sheriff for shooting his new neighbor. The motive? "Hot as it is, water's scarce," said the cowman. "And my new neighbor, he sunk a well and threw up a windmill, and sheriff, you know there's not enough breeze in that canyon to run two windmills!" No charges were filed.

When Paul Dean was writing a daily column in Phoenix he immortalized

> the motorists from Boston who stopped at Ed & Tom's 24-hour Truck Stop in Gila Bend last week. The attendant was tanned to well-done and wrinkled to a prune. His eyes were faded and shrunk to blue. His only hair were wisps of white straw. But he was spry. He hopped around the car, scratched bugs off its windshield, checked the water, kicked the tires, and handled air and water hoses like a four-armed snake charmer.

Our dude was impressed. How could this shriveled old guy be so energetic in 118-degree heat? "This climate must be very healthy," he told the gas pumper. "Guess so," the fellow replied. "Do you mind if I ask you how old you are?" "Nah," said the fellow. "Thirty-two."

But when I was writing that column, I had a hot weather story to tell, myself.

You can tell it's hot in the Valley of the Sun when people appear to be smiling. As they drive or walk the shimmering pavements, the corners of their eyes are crinkled, the skin is pouched over the cheekbones. The expression is not a smile. It is a baked-on flinch. Deceptively smiling, I opened the front door.

"In here, dear," she shouted from a back room. I went there, and she said, "The heat is all in your mind. Think of cool things like air conditioning, or water melon, or ice cream, or tinkling drinks. Let your imagination go."

I tried. "Like say I'm captain of a ship icebound in the Arctic Ocean. My jaw is jutting into the piercing gale, my hands frozen to the rail, my feet two stones on the ice-clad deck, and my breath a churning cloud as I say to the first mate, 'Mister Chillblains, be good enough to have the steward fetch me a cold bottle of beer.' "

She begged me to continue. "Or say I am driving a sled out of Fairbanks. I have lost my fur parka wrestling a polar bear. Bare-chested, I must deliver my cargo of dry ice to Nome, where a blizzard has buried the refrigerator factory." "Go on," she insisted.

"Very well. I am hired as a well digger for an expedition to Little America. Before this I was employed during winter months as a polisher of brass monkeys in a Siberian open-air pawn shop." Change the subject, she begged.

"I am a movie star. In my latest cool jazz flick my leading lady is Subzero Mercury, who portrays a frigid woman. The big scene, she gives me a frosty stare. A chill runs down my spine. My blood turns to icewater. I break out in a cold sweat. I get cold feet."

Much better, thank you. "I am an archaeologist, chiseling away the permafrost which covers the site of Eric the Red's colony in Greenland. My pick strikes a stone. My eager, blue hands brush away the frozen earth, revealing runes, which translate: 'Norsemen True Use Olaf's Frostbite Salve. Only Two Walrus Tusks, Leading Druggists.' "

She wondered if I felt cooler, and I confessed not. All in your mind, she repeated, splashing cold water on her shoulders. I asked, "How long have you been sitting in that tub?" She admitted, "I've been so intent on thinking cool things, I lost track of time."

Back when Chandler was more famous for growing hot weather cotton than high-tech computer chips, an immigrant Iowa farmer incautiously planted a field of popcorn, which reached maturity on a 115-degree day. The kernels exploded right off the ears. A flock of Marshall Humphrey's sheep in an adjoining pasture assumed the popcorn was snow, and they froze to death. Only by packing the butchered carcasses in more popcorn was the mutton kept fresh for market.

During an even worse year, Tom Sanford, fishing on Canyon Lake, lit a cigarette and set fire to half the lake. My big brother Frank had to use the other half of the lake to quench the blaze. Jerry Poole, an Okie with a master's degree in journalism, chronicled other occurrences of that season. The greasewood dried up to straw. A Casa Grande psychiatrist recommended that a newly arrived Bostonian be committed for carrying an umbrella, and when the Bostonian sued for malpractice, the doctor offered his covered parking space as a settlement. The prickly pear cactus shrank so thin there was only one side to them. The solar water heaters at Arizona State University had to be tested after sundown. At Florence, to save water, the Baptists sprinkled, the Methodists spritzed, and the Presbyterians issued rain checks. The time-and-temperature signs fell five degrees behind. A Phoenix woman doing her income tax tried to claim her air conditioner as a dependent. The heat waves were so strong, they crashed like surf. A truly bad summer, that. One mirage lasted so long, Norman Conkle bulldozed five-acre ranchettes and sold them $10 down $10 a month. The buyers doubled their money within a year.

Maybe it was during the same dry spell that Charlie Pickrell overheard an eastern tourist talking to an Arizona settler:

When Maricopa was a rail junction point from the main line into Phoenix, a tourist one morning looked out of the train and saw a wagon loaded with several barrels drawn up beside a water tank there. The Arizonan was pouring water into these barrels. The tourist, apologizing for his curiosity, inquired, "What are you going to do with the water?" The settler replied, "Taking it out to my ranch." The tourist asked, "How far is your ranch?" "Five miles," said the settler. "But wouldn't it be easier to dig a well?" "Don't make much difference," was the answer. "It's five miles, either way."

More than one southwestern rancher resorted to prayer in time of drought. According to Ernie Douglas, one Arizona cattleman put his plea to doggerel:

Dear God, my range is dry again;
Just one more rain would see us through.
But if You cannot send us rain,
A California dew will do.

Some Arizona ranchers could be forgiven their doubts about an all-knowing Lord. They still believe in Him, but sometimes wonder if He is a very good cowman. It's remindful of Big Dan H. Ming, who during the terrible drought of 1885 was asked to pray for rain in behalf of his cattlemen's association. Big Dan had the men remove their hats, and said, "Oh, Lord, I'm about to round You up for a good plain talking. Now, Lord, I ain't like those fellows who come bothering You every day. This is the first time I ever tackled You for anything, and if You will only grant this, I promise never to bother You again. We want rain, Good Lord, and we want it bad; we ask You to send us some. But if You can't or don't want to send us some, then for Christ's sake, don't make it rain up around Hooker's or Leitch's ranges, but treat us all alike. Amen."

One of the early reporters upon the Arizona scene was J. Ross Browne, who in his *Adventures in Apache Country* stated:

I have even heard complaint made that the temperature failed to show the true heat because the mercury dried up. Everything dries; wagons dry, men dry, chickens dry; there is no juice left in anything, living or dead, by the close of the summer. Officers and soldiers are supposed to walk without creaking; mules, it is said, can only bray at midnight; and I have heard it hinted that carcasses of cattle rattle inside their hides, and that snakes find difficulty in bending their bodies, and horned frogs die of apoplexy. Chickens hatched at this season, as old Fort Yumans say, come out of the shell ready cooked; bacon is eaten with a spoon; and butter must stand in the sun before the flies become dry enough to use. . . .

Things hadn't been so bad since 1869, when a journalist experienced a summer in Arizona, and wrote his editor:

The rabbits have somehow gotten the body of the hare and the ears of the ass; the frogs, the body of the toad, the horns of the stag-beetle, and the tail of the lizard. The trees fall uphill, and the lightning comes out of the ground.

Now THAT's how hot it got.

Food

If It Isn't All That Cold Why Do They Call It Chili?

I t was given to one Rolland R. Olney of Morenci, Arizona, to report upon the formulation of a new brand of southwestern beer. In the likely fictitious town of Dutchman, so named for the principal business, which was searching for the Lost Dutchman Mine, the leaders thought to expand the economic base. A group of wealthy Dutchmaniacs established a brewery. They brought off a passable lager derived from wild rye, soapweed to induce a head, and walnut shells for color.

Came a drought. The Dutchman Spring went dry. Shimmering mirages encircled the village. But the ingenious Dutchmaniacs simply ran a pipe out to the largest imaginary lake, and kept the vats filled. The new beer was much lighter than the regular beer, and it was less filling.

My New England brother-in-law, Bill Kovel, thought there was no more perfect finger food than a fried Cape Cod soft-shelled clam roll. Then I told him about the Carefree Prickly Pear Cactus Sandwich. Slabs of prickly pear cactus on plain, store-bought bread: you can eat your sandwich and pick your teeth at the same time.

Then there's the Chuck Sherrill steak dinner. Chuck is supposed to have flown into Phoenix from his ranch in Pleasant Valley and ordered a well-done steak, a bottle of whiskey, and a hound dog.

"A dog?"

"To eat the steak," said Chuck. In explaining what might be taken as antisocial behavior in some quarters, Chuck ventured that town restaurants never seemed capable of cooking beef truly well done; he'd have to send it back with the kindly critique—"Chihuahua! We've had cows hurt worse'n that and got well."

Chuck was the same livestock grower who fired his ramrod for returning from town with twelve quarts of whiskey and a loaf of bread. Reason for dismissal: "What in hell are we going to do with all that bread?"

Believe that or not, the following was sworn to by the late cartoonist Kearney Egerton of *The Arizona Republic* newspaper:

The scene was Chicago in the winter of '38 or '39. Windy, wet, cold. The hour was a few minutes before 7 p.m., when Chicagoans sloshing along the sidewalk near the downtown cluster of hospitals and medical schools were startled to see two young men in the flamboyant uniform of the New Mexico State Police emerge from a taxicab and dash into an apartment building.

The frostbitten bystanders may have assumed that the two officers, obviously of Mexican lineage, had pursued a fugitive all the way from Tularosa or Socorro into the Windy City. They were wrong. The policemen were about to lay hands, not upon a fleeing felon, but upon *tostadas compuestas, quesadillas, chiles rellenos, jamon,* and full-dress *burritos.*

Here is what happened: there was a small enclave of southwesterners attending the schools of medicine and dentistry in Chicago. As the soggy heat of summer gave way to the dark and cloudy cold of winter, the scholars' thoughts turned unanimously to Mexican food. The colder they got, the more they thought about it, and there is no creature more miserable than a southwesterner who is beset by sleet and deprived of chili.

Then the mother of one came to their rescue. She mailed unto him, on a regular basis, C.A.R.E. packages that contained corn tortillas (sealed in fruit jars for freshness), cans of salsa, green chilies and *jalapenos,* and blocks of dehydrated chili from which you sawed off as much as you needed and tossed into a pot with water, salt, bacon, fat, garlic and oregano, and then you simmered it until it became a thick, fragrant sauce.

Anyway, the budding medico (he later became an associate dean of the Northwestern University Medical School) would summon his colleagues to regular repasts of enchiladas, tacos, and the like, and they would all return to their studies of anatomical malfunctions with renewed vigor. The students heard that the two young officers were enrolled in Northwestern's traffic institute—and that they were suffering from malnutrition. The next time the students orchestrated a Mexican smorgasbord, the policemen were invited and they responded with the zeal noted above.

"Johnny! Luis!" they shouted as they burst into the apartment. "You have saved our lives!"

Such belief is not unusual in the Southwest. When Europeans arrived in the New World, unfamiliar foods awaited them: pumpkins, peanuts, corn, avocados, potatoes, tomatoes, beans. And at least three magnificent flavors: chocolate, vanilla, chili. Today's true chili-heads are of a mind that the *capsicum* alone was worth the trip. Chile breeders now differentiate among more than a hundred varieties, ranging in bite from the mild canning pimiento to fiery *chiletepines.* Thanks to the robust but civilized flavor of the adaptable Anaheim, chili consumption in the United States is estimated to be increasing fifteen percent per year.

Although certainly not the only pusher, Joe Jordan generally is credited with smuggling *capsicum annum* and its piquant relations north of Van Buren Street in Phoenix. And, Joe insists, besides tasting immorally delicious, the stuff is next to a wonder drug—raises body temperature, relieves cramps, stimulates digestion, improves complexion, reverses inebriation, cures hangover, soothes gout, and increases passion. Joe would have us remember that Albert von Szent-Gyorgi won the Nobel Prize in Physiology and Medicine in 1937 by isolating from red peppers the scurvy-fighting ascorbic acid, better known as vitamin C. You could look it up. Or ask Louise Dewald.

But again, history may hold back essence. When a fully developed cold snap tears through Freezeout Canyon in mid-

January, cowboys caught in the blizzard make their fires from pitchy knots pried out of four-hundred-year-old ponderosa pine snags. Sizzling hot as the fires rage, they freeze solid anyway, and the camp cook grinds up the flames into chili powder. They've got to be careful with that spice—it will melt a Dutch oven! And draw blisters on the coldest banker's heart....

What to put in with chili ever has promulgated controversies greater than politics, sex, and religion combined. In 1864, in the territorial capital of Prescott, one restaurant's entire printed menu: "Breakfast, fried venison and chili; dinner, roast venison and chili, or chili and beans; supper, chili." Beef was not included, because the chef could not find a neighbor's stray steer that day.

Into modern times the formula for a proper bowl of brimstone defies consensus. Jeanne Croft of *New Mexico Magazine* once proposed chili MEATBALLS! Mother of God, that is Latin food! Pass the chimichangas, Brutus. Joe Cooper recommended olive oil. Jim Beard, for all of his encyclopedic knowledge of New World food, always was a tomato-and-bean chili freak, and he actually advised freeborn Americans to ladle that concoction over rice. Dorothee Polson has written authoritatively on the Chili Appreciation Society (International), and great chili cookoffs at Wichita Falls and Terlingua, Texas; Rosamond, California; and Phoenix, Arizona; but (perhaps wisely) she withheld stating a preference for carne cubed, ground, or shredded. Dorothee did, however, expose Ladybird Johnson as an advocate of TUNA chili, which says a lot for encouraging her total commitment to roadside beauty.

Fame seems no guarantee of wisdom. Carroll Shelby wasn't above serving chili with corn bread and cole slaw. The matriarch of another western racing family, Mom Unser, smiled upon pork. For a while, the adored chili addict was Elizabeth Taylor, until the world caught on that she was tolerating parsley by the fistful, monosodium glutamate by the cup, and vast shovels of BLACK pepper. Polly Bergen would toss in ground meat and a dollop of vinegar. Betty Ford, RED beans. Though it's hard to believe, Betsy Balsley of the *Los Angeles Times* documented a Texas Hotel Chili served on oyster crackers. Senator Barry Goldwater would not forego pinto beans (in your heartburn you know he's wrong). Rosalyn Carter preferred tomato PASTE, which could explain a one-term presidency. Even Arizona chili master C.V. Wood Jr. (he purchased London Bridge to transplant to Lake Havasu City) published a twenty-five ingredient concoction including chopped celery, a stewing chicken, a spoon of monosodium glutamate, the squeeze of a lime, and a cup of beer. There are fanatics who would pass federal laws against garlic, or even a hint of chili without cumin. Some actually savor the rubbery crimson paste brushed on frozen dinners, and some, like Jim Cook, want their fix "hotter than ninety-nine-cent jumper cables." It may have hastened the demise of Frank X. Tolbert (*A Bowl of Red*) when some dangerously demented Creoles started a chili pot with a broth of chicken backs, ham hocks, and crab boil. Obscenity laws forbid the mention of ingredients proposed by Australians, North African tribesmen, and Hank Rosenthal, a Texan who moved to Alaska and spends far too much time in Kotzebue. Giles Goswick used to jerk cougar with which to feed his hounds on the trail, and as a gag, once fed some to cow waddy Port Parker. He liked it.

Otherwise, passable chili has transformed elk, raccoon, opossum, burro (elevated to interplanetary fame by former Congressman Sam Steiger), squirrel, musk hog, moose, bear, horse (much preferred by nineteenth-century American Indians), quail, mourning dove, squab, armadillo, javelina (the official song of the Arizona National Guard is entitled, "Have a Javelina, Lena"), salt pork, antelope, mutton, Hoover hog (the only protein in Official Oklahoma Chili), duck (once done in a wok by Woodruff De Silva), hot dogs, Campbell's Soup, and dirty jokes (the comic writer H. Allen Smith produced an entire book of them heard at chili cook-offs). Frank Malone and Dudley Lynch can swear to all of the above.

Ordinarily, the libations of New Spain might rate a chapter separate from food folklore, but the watershed works of Dr. Iris H. Wilson seem right to mention here. She illuminated for posterity a treatise executed in 1791 by Don Antonio Pineda, serving as chief of natural history for an ambitious survey of the economy of the province. As Dr. Wilson tells us, Pineda analyzed, though he may not have imbibed, seventy-seven distinct native beverages of varying degrees of intoxicating powers. A sampler: *aguardiente* (distilled from grapes); *cerveza* (barley beer); *chinguirito* (fermented honey); *mezcal* (drawn from fermented succulent); *nochocle* (fermented liquids including prickly pear juice); *pozole* (soured popcorn); *resoli* (spiced liquor of rice, beans, and barley); *sidra* (hard apple cider); *tuba* (distilled coconut juice); and *zardagita* (citron punch). As may be supposed, such a tradition promulgated an agenda of cures. Now, a reasonable boast: hangovers by custom today are dealt with most dramatically in the far Southwest, and within Mexico.

Journalists know of these things. Some years ago a national columnist named Westbrook Pegler awoke *muy crudo* on New Year's Day. His contract called for a thousand words. He wrote, "Oh, my God!" three hundred and thirty-three times and signed it "Peg."

Thus prospers a worldwide competition in cures. The Koreans inhale a stew of beef blood, onions, and peppers. Note, peppers. Hungover Hungarians swear by sauerkraut soup. Russians, salted cucumber juice. Frenchmen, ice packs. In greater America, maybe the less said the better about stale Coca-Cola, the Ramos Fizz, the Pearly Oyster, the Morning Mourning, and San Francisco's Dirty Mother.

No. Trust the Southwest. Menudo, spicy soup of tripe and hominy, is the Mexican "one for the road." In Agua Prieta on the border abaft Douglas, overindulgers down *enchiladas con huevos* smothered in warm tequila. The Prairie Oyster begins with a can of chilled tomatoes, and grows upon a tablespoon of steak sauce, a dash of Tabasco, and a raw egg. It is consumed neat. Most popular south by west is a mix of grapefruit juice, tequila, and salt. Then, the Bull Shot (jigger of mescal on the rocks, smothered in beef consomme) and El Toro (equal parts orange soda and beer), both with a smallish dash of Tabasco. As implied, Americans elsewhere have sought relief in drinks named Comet's Tail, Mule's Ear, Roman Candle, Frog's Blood, and Tomato Zombie. Southwesterners with small pity embrace the view that other provincials who swallow Southern Comfort, a dulcet compound of old bourbon, oranges, and peaches that tests a hundred proof, have the right, nay, the duty, to suffer.

One more word on chili. The closest this correspondent ever came to an altercation with a Texan (aside from that ugly exchange of inferred parentage with an eighty-five-year-old grandmother on Houston's 610 Freeway), was with Calvin Clyde Jr., a newspaperman of Tyler. He fancied himself the Chili Poet of the Piney Woods, in evidence:

> You chop a heap o' onions fine,
>   and add small chunks o'meat
> (Leftover goat from Sunday
>   when the padre came to eat).
> Next, throw in lots o' peppers,
>   all browned in jaguar grease. . . .

Not at all bad for Tejano jingling, but do take note of the last word quoted. Grease. In the most commendable fraternal spirit, I pointed out that Texas chili with or without beans usually was a tad greasy. This tendency explains the all-but-universal understanding of the menu term, Texas Jail Chili, with all three words required, as in Boston Cream Pie.

Warming to my benevolent mission, I sent colleague Clyde a list of particulars.

How, once in Harlingen, I could find no name-brand oil, filled the crankcase with twenty bowls of red, which required no change for fifty thousand miles.

How, covering a ship launching in Galveston, I asked the sledgeman what he used on the ways. He said, "Chili."

How, Amarillo has a secret contingency plan for converting refineries from crude to roadside reserves.

How, outside Lufkin, they slay unwanted weeds with surplus chili.

How, as a boy I had controlled my cowlick with Lone Star Pomade.

How, once touring U.S. Route 90 from Uvalde to San Antonio, I was grateful for the detour dressed with red tallow.

How, a Texas chili tanker broke up at Corpus, and no detergent known could disperse the slick.

How, after that disaster, Texas City passed a stiff ordinance on distances required between chili tanks.

And how, at Llano, a chili dipper can float seven distinct layers of grease of varying hue and viscosity, as in the building of a pousse-cafe. But the minimum portion per customer is fifty-five gallons.

Clyde regrettably exhibited an ungrateful streak. He implied that the low fat content of Arizona chili had something to do with the leanness of desert dogs. One Wickford P. (Wick) Fowler of Austin invited me to a Whooping Crane hunt, at a time when there were only forty-nine batches of that endangered chili to be made. And the aforementioned Frank Tolbert was incited to call me, in the *Dallas Morning News,* "a crockery-eyed, whiskery, curmudgeonous, old tantrum of a codger." I thought to sue, for at the time I was clean shaven.

Time passes. Passions subside. We should be grateful for Tolbert's little Bible, *A Bowl of Red,* even if in it Frank X. summons the shade of Will Rogers to testify in behalf of Texas.

> The late humorist and film actor...said that he judged a town by the chili it served. He sampled chili in hundreds of little towns, especially in Texas and Oklahoma. He kept a box score. Will finally concluded that the finest chili of his experience was in a small cafe in Coleman, Texas. The ingredients for this concoction included "mountain oyster from a bull, not a calf, raised on the slopes of the Santa Anna Mountains...."

But even beloved wits have been known to slip. Arch Napier of Albuquerque, New Mexico, mustered legions of like-minded chili heads when he wrote a letter that was printed in *Life Magazine* March 21, 1969:

> Sirs: You are giving this exciting food a bad name by linking it to the crude stuff served in Texas. Texas chili is a test of endurance, primarily useful in terrorizing tourists and fracturing oil wells. Last year, the Texans had a kind of chili cooking contest—conducted like a shoot-out—and it was publicized on the front pages along with crimes and disasters. When New Mexico chili cuisine is discussed in our newspapers, it is usually carried on the Art and Music pages.

Politicians

A Loose Gathering of Variegated Strays

"Facts are like cattle," Charlie Pickrell often said. "You can't judge a herd until the last cow is in the pen." We never seem capable of rounding up every last political cow, and lacking all the facts, we are left with legends, as this one, delivered without notes by Senator Henry Fountain Ashurst:

The glorious character of the Thirteenth Legislature was Mickey Stewart of Flagstaff.... He was in court one day defending a man accused of shooting three times at another man. He said, "Gentlemen of the jury, do you blame my client? This man was advancing upon him, hurling vile EPITAPHS at him as he came."

The District Attorney interrupted, "I'm sure, Mr. Stewart, you mean vile EPITHETS, not EPITAPHS."

"No," said Counselor Stewart, "I don't mean epithets. I know what I mean. I mean epitaphs. The law does not permit you to strike or shoot a man when he hurls epithets at you, but in our western life, in our pioneer world, when a man comes at you hurling EPITAPHS, then it's time for you to finish him."

Ashurst likewise is the source of a biographical peek at his colleague, Senator Ralph H. Cameron:

He didn't waste time in words. He said I wasted time in words. One morning he received a letter from a constituent when he was a delegate to Congress. It said, "Dear Cameron, now that you're in Congress and we're from Christian homes, we want you to get us an appropriation for a church." Cameron wired back, "I can't get you an appropriation for a church. You can't dip into public funds for church matters. Besides, Congress doesn't know anything about religion. And secondly, what you need there is not a church. What you need there is a jail. I'll get you a jail."

A public official continuing the good humor of Ashurst is Arizona's veteran Congressman Morris (call me Mo) Udall, who may gain more attention with his book *Just Laughing About It This Morning* than he ever did with his tries at the presidency. The title of the book of twelve hundred funnies, gassers, and anecdotes comes from his 1976 experience in the New Hampshire primaries. He walked into a barbershop and gushed, "Hi, I'm Mo Udall. I have just announced that I am running for president." The barber replied, "Yep. We were just laughing about it this morning."

Depending upon one's political loyalties, Congressman Sam Steiger served through the 1960s and 1970s either as the rankest of Republican reactionaries or the ablest of Constitutional fundamentalists. But love him or leave him, Sam was never dull. He relished telling how, late in a tough election, carburetor ice forced down his light airplane in a cold, remote, barren, and radio-blind Arizona canyon. To keep from freezing, Sam and his pilot were obliged to burn bales of his campaign literature. No loss, probably, because as Sam told it, he eventually flew on to Clifton, a mining town ninety-nine percent Democrat. Sam quoted a Mexican miner: "I sure am mad at my brother because of you." Why? Steiger wondered—"Your brother has been dead for twenty years!" "That is true, Mr. Steiger," the man answered, "but the last time you ran for Congress, he came back to life and voted for your opponent seven times, and my brother, he never dropped by the house once to say hello."

Another Arizona politician with a quick wit: Barry Goldwater. Once an editor suggested that the most famous native son of Arizona likely was not Goldwater but Geronimo. A strained look crossed the features of Senator Goldwater, also Arizona-born and the state's only candidate for the presidency. "Well," the editor hurried on, "all over the world did you ever hear of somebody bailing out of an airplane, pulling the parachute ripcord, and yelling, GOLD-WATER?" The senator mulled that over, and conceded. "You're right. Geronimo is the most famous Arizonan—ever."

When he finally was allowed in 1969 to go to Vietnam—having been denied permission for years by the Democratic administration—Goldwater rattled the nerves of his security-conscious aides by pooh-poohing dangers. Mortared at Da Nang, Goldwater slept through it. Cautioned about appearing unguarded in an ordinary sedan in riot-torn Saigon, Goldwater quipped, "You forget, in Washington every day I go to work in an unsecured government village." And deep in the jungles of the Central Highlands during a lull in combat, a cavalry sergeant rose from his muddy foxhole to shout down the barbed wire, "Barry, I voted for you in '64, and I'd vote for you again!" Goldwater turned to a companion and muttered, "Hell, obviously, I was running in the wrong precinct...." But the man who was rejected 49 to 1 by the United States (Goldwater DID carry his home state) must have derived some gratification when, after the election, an old Arizona rancher moseyed up to him and confided, "Barry, they said if I voted for you in 1964, we'd be in a land war in Asia within six months. So, I voted for you, and SURE ENOUGH...."

When Burton Barr gave up his most powerful post of house majority leader to run for governor, he claimed, tongue-in-cheek, that he had to hire a lunatic to telephone his house two or three times a night and cuss him out just so he could get some sleep. Having made his political decision, Barr now may mull over that mother's apocryphal lament, "Once I had three sons. And they have all disappeared. One joined a cloistered order. Another was lost at sea. And the third ran for governor of Arizona, and won."

Let us reserve a warm spot for Arizona legislator Patrick W. O'Reilly who justified for all time the high salaries of professors. Most of the Arizona legislators that year were ranchers, who could not understand why anyone should be paid handsomely, fulltime, for teaching only a few hours a day. "A professor is much like a bull," O'Reilly explained. "We must not consider the amount of time he spends, but the importance of what he does."

The Southwest's greatest real-life liar, at least until modern times, was James Addison Reavis, nicknamed the Baron of Arizona. In 1887, the flamboyant Reavis laid claim to twelve million acres of Arizona and New Mexico. Basis for the claim, an old Spanish grant, was recognized by the U.S. government, and titles to lands in a tract three times the size of Connecticut were clouded. For six years Reavis extracted use fees from squatters—fifty thousand dollars from a railroad, and another fifty thousand from a mine, plus numerous smaller amounts. The grandiose scam eventually was debunked by a small town printer who detected modern-day type faces and watermarks in Reavis's spurious documents. Reavis went to prison in Santa Fe.

The mainline railroad reached Tucson in 1880, inducing such euphoria, telegrams were sent around the world, including one, "To his Holiness, the Pope of Rome, Italy. The Mayor of Tucson begs the honor of reminding Your Holiness that this ancient and honorable pueblo was founded by the Spaniards under the sanctions of the Church more than three centuries ago, and to inform Your Holiness that a railroad from San Francisco now connects us with the Christian world. . . ." It is suspected that more sophisticated Tucson citizens intercepted the message, for the answering wire read: "His Holiness the Pope. . . sends his benediction, but for his own satisfaction would ask, where in hell is Tucson? [Signed] Antonelli."

Prescott lost the capital to Phoenix in 1889, but the suspicion persists that the culprit was a Prescott booster who failed to answer roll call. He couldn't attend that day's session because a "lady of the evening" had swallowed his glass eye. That incident well may have given rise to the widely held and oft-repeated comment that the Arizona legislature is the only state institution run by the inmates.

Bingo Johnson, rawboned timbersetter, and Ned White, a sensitive poet, were running for Bisbee justice. White mounted a powder box and addressed a knot of Brewery Gulch drinkers/voters: "Gentlemen of this revered arroyo, I am a Candidate for the high office of justice of the peace. It is a position of responsibility and determination. Order is the primary law of civilization. . . ." At this moment Bingo Johnson rose and struck White a stunning blow. White picked himself up and concluded his campaign speech, "and self-preservation is the first law of nature. Gentlemen, I withdraw!"

For the year Phoenix was laid out, *The Prescott Miner* published a list of four hundred pioneers killed (two burned alive) by Indians, and mostly Apaches blamed. That was also the year of the Camp Grant Massacre. Bands of mercenaries under white direction fell upon a village of sleeping Apache women and children prisoners-of-war, in an orgy of revenge, rape, and mutilation. On hearing that a hundred died, President Grant exclaimed, "Purely murder!" There was a trial, of course. The all-white jury was out nineteen minutes. Not guilty. The only local criticism: the press faulted the jury's "protracted deliberation."

The first town hall, courthouse, and justice's office in Phoenix was an adobe serving also as a butcher shop. Pete Holcomb would kill a steer and hang the quarters. Customers furnishing their own knives would cut off what they wanted, at twenty-five cents a pound. One beef kept Phoenix fed for a week.

Phoenix's first election of a sheriff was a notable failure, inasmuch as one candidate, climaxing a bitter argument, fatally shot the other.

Headline, *Phoenix Herald*, 1879: "CARNIVAL OF CRIME! A Bloody Week in Phoenix Ends with a Grand Neck-tie Party. Six Persons Launched on Their Journey Down the Dark River. Reckless Romero Madly Rushes to His Doom, Takes Three Pistol Balls with Him. John La Bar Stabbed Fatally by a Drunken Ruffian. Jesus Figero Pistoled on the Gila and Another Mexican Knifed at Seymour. McClosky and Keller Hurried Hellward at the End of a Rope."

It falls to Lester (Budge) Ruffner to perpetuate the better yarns of Yavapai. Such as, the cowboy at Camp Creek who perused a Phoenix newspaper and concluded, "That Doe family must be a hell of a mean outfit, because every time I read about them, they are in trouble."

Arizona never had a hanging judge to rank with Roy Bean of Texas, but that judge's biographer did retire to Tucson. Dr. C.L. Sonnichsen in *Roy Bean: Law West of the Pecos*, tells us Judge Bean's rationale regarding divorces: "Heck, I married 'em, didn't I. Then I got the right to un-marry 'em. A man has the right to rectify his own errors, ain't he?" Dr. Sonnichsen documents the impeccable Judge Bean logic in pronouncing a corpse guilty of carrying concealed weapons, and imposing a forty dollar fine, which by coincidence exactly equalled the amount the dead man had in his pockets.

But according to Ruffner, Prescott's pioneer judge John J. Hawkins also deserves a historical footnote, in that he presided over Arizona's briefest mistrial. Budge: "One day a trial was to begin for an illiterate, mentally slow defendant. The judge entered the courtroom and the bailiff ordered everyone to stand. And when the judge sat down, the bailiff ordered everyone to do the same. One man remained standing near the front of the room. Hawkins peered down from the bench and asked, 'Are you the defendant, sir?' The man answered, 'No, judge, I'm the guy who stole the horse.'"

In time, Judge Hawkins went into private practice. More Ruffner: "One of his clients was a local madam who was opening a new and exclusive establishment. She wanted a proper name to project an image of elegance. Hawkins was an educated man, and he told the woman he would study some of the world's great literature to come up with a name. And he did. Above the expensive oak door, in a window of etched crystal, was printed the name, Caveat Emptor."

From one of Arizona's most respected supreme court justices, Levi S. Udall, is transmitted the anecdote involving a pioneer magistrate in Apache County. Evidence in a case overwhelmingly placed the defendant away from the scene of the crime, and the prosecutor capitulated. "Your honor, this trial has to stop right here. The alibi has been fully established." The judge responded, "I think so myself. I say, what is the penalty for an alibi?"

Bill Ridgway of Willcox enjoyed the honesty of an old horse wrangler named Cyclone. Once, a territorial judge introduced Cyclone by his alias, and Cyclone exploded, "Everybody calls you a dignified old goat, judge, but nobody introduces you that way."

Some Arizona cases never reached court. A vigilance committee dragged suspected robber John Heath from his cell and hanged him outside the Tombstone Courthouse (now a state park) on February 22, 1884. A hastily empaneled coroner's jury took note of the lack of oxygen at high altitude and attributed the death to "emphysema of the lungs, self-inflicted or otherwise."

Pete Kitchen is the Arizona pioneer (although elsewhere it can be

Jim Bridger or Pecos Bill) who lost his favorite horse to a band of thieves. Pete followed the trail and recovered the pony. In the process he took a prisoner south of the border. In desperate need of sleep on the ride home, Pete made camp. To prevent the suspect's escape, Pete left him in the saddle, his neck attached by a lariat to a tree limb.

"And you know," Pete afterward would confide, "that damned horse during the night walked off and left that fellow hanging there!" A kindred legend has an eastern dude asking how the wrangler's father died. "Fell through some scaffolding," said the wrangler. "He was hanged."

Tom Fulbright, cow-country counselor, was invited by a pair of Arizona judges to summarize his qualifications for a good judge. Tom said, "First, I want a judge who will listen to me. For, in most instances, a lawyer who has prepared his case knows more about it than any presiding judge. I expect him to hear me until I am through. Last, if he knows a little law, while it isn't necessary, it does no harm."

Miners and prospectors salted Arizona history with high-grade legend, none more compelling than that of the Lost Dutchman, Jacob Waltz (it's spelled that way on his Phoenix tombstone). "Beware, lest you, too, succumb to the lure," warns an official state highway sign near the foreboding face of the Superstition Range. Waltz himself guarded his privacy yet fostered rumors of Spanish gold; before his death in 1891, Waltz presented a gift of a box of nuggets to a friend. A few who tried to follow him never were seen again. Into the late twentieth century, the quest for the Dutchman's bonanza has led to perhaps fifty deaths, most of them attributed to exhaustion and exposure. And as far as is known, Oren Arnold, writer, is the only one who found a pot of gold: fourteen thousand dollars in royalties for a brief booklet he produced in two hours.

The ever-resourceful Charlie Pickrell kept fresh the tale of a prospector who set off on what was to be an extended trip, but returned to town within a few days, barefoot. He explained: "My jacks were newly shod, and I had hobnails in my boots, and we got stuck on a field of magnetic iron. Lucky for me, I was able to untie my laces and step out of my boots. Now if some of you fellows will help me pull my animals free, I'll be much obliged." That may have been the same prospector whose jackass ate some sticks of dynamite. Blew up the house, wrecked the corral, killed the wife, touched off a landslide. And complained the prospector, "That burro is not feeling well, either."

Then, southwestern "so-o-o" stories.

Fed poorly, cowboys riding for the Chiricahua Cattle Company were so-o-o thin, three had to stand side by side to cast a shadow.

Canyon, so-o-o deep, took two men to see to the bottom of it.

Cowboy, so-o-o fast, when he turned down the bunkhouse lantern he was in his bedroll before it got dark.

Chino Valley soil, so-o-o rich, a barn of cottonwood poles took root and grew and by nightfall the new barn was two stories high.

Earthquake, so-o-o devastating, it improved forty percent of downtown Yuma.

White Mountains creek, so-o-o crooked, when you jumped across it, you landed on the same side.

Holbrook saloon, so-o-o tough, a customer when complimenting the bartender on the new sawdust on the floor was told, "That ain't sawdust; that's last night's furniture."

Cornville scarecrow, so-o-o scary, crows bring back corn they stole two years ago.

Wall clock in a Whiskey Row tavern, so-o-o old, the shadow of the pendulum, swinging back and forth, has worn a hole in the back of the case.

Water in Buckeye, so-o-o hard, folks had to chew it before they could swallow it.

Big Jim Griffith considers himself a specialist in stories of the Mexican borderlands. He says tall tales serve to defuse international tensions and make possible social commentary. Consider the FBI agent who crossed the line and cornered a suspected Mexican robber of an Arizona bank. Through his Mexican interpreter, the agent demanded, "Where did you hide the money?" The answer, "I forgot." Whereupon the agent drew his pistol and instructed his interpreter: "Tell him that if he does not tell me, I will shoot him." And the suspect said in Spanish, "The money is in a coffee can under the fourth floor board in the hall closet of my brother's house on Via del Rio in Magdalena." "What did he say?" asked the agent. The interpreter stated, "Senor, he says he is ready to die like a man!"

Farming in fertile, arid Arizona does present challenges. In the Casa

Grande Valley toward Eloy, third-generation dust bowl descendants ingeniously developed dehydrated water. It weighs practically nothing, so costs little to pump. Drought-resistant alfalfa naturally relished it, and cattle grazing in such pastures needed only to be sliced as chipped beef. Cotton geneticists picked up on the idea, and that was the origin of drip-dry shirts.

Never solved, the problem with melons of all sizes. They grow so fast, so big, they wear out dragging on the ground. A nail keg broke and spilled at Wellton, and resulted in a crop of crowbars. Only takes seven Chandler grapefruits to make a dozen.

Indians. They were here first, and had a disastrous immigration policy. Theirs were difficult times, more than we know, yet we have in many of our portrayals added the insult: stolid, dull, humorless. But if you are so fortunate to live any time at all with Indian people, you learn they are quick to laughter, especially if a paleface is the victim.

"Do any Indians still send up smoke signals?" I once asked Pete Homer, chairman of the Colorado River tribes. "Sure," said Pete. "I do. On hot fire, throw wet green leaves. Then send up one white puff, and three black puffs."

"What's it mean?" I asked, stepping into Pete's trap.

"Nothing," he said. "But the Bureau of Indian Affairs requires two copies of everything."

The moderator at a governmental workshop in Tucson tried to hurry discussion. He asked Tom Dodge, superintendent of the San Carlos agency, to give an answer in thirty seconds.

"To summarize," said Tom. "Ugh."

And then there was the Washington official researching the Mandans, a tribe of American aborigines with blue eyes, blonde hair, and light skin. "Could it have been," the white man wondered, "that the Mandans were started by the Welsh or Norse or some other white race?"

An Arizona Hopi Indian shot back, "Did it ever occur to you that possibly the Mandans sailed overseas and founded the white race and sailed back?"

Another sharpshooter, Marshall Tome, Navajo newspaperman, in a talk to a luncheon of Indian leaders, "Anybody can see that our worst public relations is the presence of Indians in Gallup and Winslow and Flagstaff and other towns along U.S. Route 66. So I tell my Indian friends, you shouldn't buy a bottle and sit in the middle of a transcontinental highway. When you do that, you are just another drunk Indian.

"No. You guys should go down to the San Juan River and set aside a big piece of the reservation, and put some irrigation on that land, and make grass and trees grow on that land. Then, you should put a chain link fence around the whole place. A fence so high that an Indian can't climb out. Now, just inside the main gate you should build a beautiful club house. You could have your own liquor store, right there. Then you guys should get some golf bags to carry your bottles in. So you walk around under the trees and drink some wine, and get a little crazy in the head, but you can't climb that fence. And when you fall down, you don't land in the middle of the freeway. You fall down on that nice, soft grass. A friendly Indian policeman picks you up and puts you in the club house to sleep.

"No longer will you be a drunk Indian. As in the white world, you will be a SPORTSMAN."

The Irresistible Plot Meets the Immovable Man

Midway through the morning it was obvious we were going to be skunked. Into the sixth hour we had drowned two dozen live salamanders, lost a few heirloom plugs, and paved the bottom of Bartlett Reservoir with black plastic worms. And all that clung to our stringer was a coat of rust.

Not that the situation was so grim. The Arizona sun blazed. A soft, cool breeze kept the skiff drifting down the points. Nearby, ducks practiced touch-and-go landings. At hand were sandwiches and beer. It was time for dozing and dreaming.

Says I, "Buddy, one hell of a great idea for coining a bundle of money just struck me."

"Sure," answers Buddy, not opening his eyes.

"No kidding," I insist. "It's a plot for a blockbuster television miniseries or a film classic. Here we are today with a couple of tackle boxes bulging with lures that do not catch fish. Multiply us by thirty million American anglers. That amounts to a tremendous potential audience."

My companion stirs. "Go on," he says.

"Let me just wing it. The hero is a quiet, easy-going Joe, and his hobby is lures. One night out in the garage, Joe, like Goodyear with rubber, accidentally drops a half-whittled wooden plug onto his son's plastic insect-making set, which then dumps over onto a feather duster. Joe retrieves the lure, which now is a wild thing—eccentric, colorfully doped, and grossly fletched. And instead of just chucking it, Joe tosses it into his tackle box.

"So one day Joe is fishing and like us, no luck . . . and for no good reason he snaps on the oddball lure and casts it over into a cove."

"Joe catches a fish," says my buddy.

"A great-granddad mossy-back of a fish. And another, and another. It is truly, The Irresistible Lure."

My buddy picks up the story thread. "Joe is no fool. He goes home and makes models of many sizes. Then he experiments. And sure enough, every time he casts he catches a sunfish or a marlin or something in between."

"Exactly. Joe protects the lure with an ironclad patent, takes out a loan from the credit union, and sets up a production line. Then he sends out a few freebies to the outdoor writers. They would compose a Shakespearean sonnet about a no-account lure, so you can imagine what they say about one that is irresistible. Demand is created overnight."

"A hundred bucks a copy. Why not? It replaces every plug in the tackle box, plus the tackle box. Joe's gross in the first year is three billion dollars. His production cost is a penny a plug. To make up the costs of distribution and overhead, he negotiates foreign licenses.

"Meantime, chaos. Fish and game biologists are going bananas trying to keep the lakes and streams stocked. Sporting goods stores are folding like paper tents. Manufacturers of all other lures are bellying up.

"Lawsuits against Joe get nowhere. Congress holds hearings, and thirty million fishermen protest. A president moves to ban the lure, and is driven from office. In backing Joe unanimously, Supreme Court Justices confess they have all bought the irresistible lure. The entire economy is thrown out of kilter. Joe suddenly has more clout than the Bass Brothers and the Hunt Family. He hires L.L. Bean as a stock boy."

"Uh-oh," says my buddy. "What about counterfeit imports?"

"No problem. Only Joe knows the secret combination."

My buddy wonders, "Could the system stand that strain? Wouldn't the Establishment find some way to foil Joe?"

"Not at all," I explain. "Joe is the epitome of the American dream, that every boy or girl has an equal chance to grow up and accidentally discover a high-demand, cheaply made monopoly item. The nation's faith is restored."

"That's beautiful," says my buddy. "For the last scene of your movie I can see the camera kind of low, tilt-angle, and Jimmy Stewart as Joe in hip boots and creel, marching to martial music, and a patriotic montage flickering over the sky. When are you going to write the script?"

"I'm not. I've changed my mind. I don't want to write about The Irresistible Lure. I want to invent it."

Generally appreciated, Arizona is cowboy land. Also obvious, Arizona can be fishing paradise. Not so well known, cowboys hugely enjoy fishing. THEIR way.

In 1960 on the Coronado Trail Ride were three genuine cowboys—Herbert Nichols, cattle inspector; Harold Filleman, rancher; and Marshall Simms, one of the few state senators who could shoe a horse. We had packed a hundred miles into the primitive forests lying north of Clifton and west of U.S. Route 666. One lazy day in camp Simms said, "Let's go fishing," and Nichols echoed, "Let's saddle up!"

This struck me, city dude, as funny. Here we were on Reservation Creek, where the trout lined up in the eddies like cordwood, and only a quarter of a mile from Black River, where even larger rainbows lurked.

"You cowboys will go to all that trouble to catch horses and saddle them, just to save a few steps, and when you get down to the river, you'll have to tie up the animals and worry about them, just to save a few steps. Heck, let's walk," said I.

Nichols looked at me with pity. He said he guessed I never went fishing cowboy style.

So we rode to the river. Nichols and Filleman were mounted on mules, and when they reached the river, they kicked the animals into the center of the stream of snowmelt. They tied knots in the reins and dropped them over the saddle horns. They baited and cast, and pretty soon a couple of trout were landed, or, more accurately, saddled.

The cowboys favored a rig to give a fly fisherman the shudders. They tied about twelve feet of line to a cane pole. At the end of a short leader they fastened a No. 1 hook, and about a foot from the hook, they wrapped the line with lead foil peeled from the necks of whiskey bottles.

It's different—cowboy style. The mules and mountain ponies were sure of foot in the river...in fact, seemed to enjoy the swim across deep holes. Saddle-high, a fisherman can make championship casts to far corners. (The only looming catastrophe is hooking your horse in the rump. Look out!) A ten-incher snapped up the first black gnat I offered, and my horse, Champagne, trained to cowboy fishing, headed for shore. Soon we were back in camp with fishes to feed the multitudes.

The cowboys did not use creels. They tied their fish to their saddle strings.

And at this point, I think these cowboys tried to fool the dude.

"Once in a while," said Nichols, "I hook into a really big trout, and I throw a dally around my saddle horn and let the mule pull the fish to shore. If the fish is REALLY big, Filleman will hook the head and I'll hook the tail, team style. A legal tie with the piggin' string is two fins and the tail."

So much for truth.

Ernie Gay of the White Mountain Country Club tells of a stranger who asked to be taken onto Luna Lake. Ernie rowed out to a quiet nook, wrapped a stick of dynamite onto a brick bat, lit the fuse, tossed it overboard, and after the explosion, selected the ten largest trout from the lake surface.

"Very interesting," said the stranger. "I am the game ranger."

Ernie nonchalantly taped another charge to another brick, tossed the bomb into the ranger's lap, and asked: "Now are you going to arrest me, or get to fishing?"

Dynamite. That was the salvation of a bounty hunter over on the Blue after a calf-killer bear. He ran short of bullets and left a stick of honey-covered explosive in his trail. Mr. Bear was not the first big fellow to lose his head over a sweet little thing.

Then salt. Mark Twain, from a Kentucky source, retold that yarn about a hunter so keen he had to pack salt in his bullets to keep the meat from spoiling while he hiked the long distance to the kill. Arizona hunters sharpen those bullets and pack them with pepper so that by the time they hike the extreme range, the meat is already made into jerky. One old Arizona boy followed the path of his bullet and encountered a smoked turkey, two cured hams, and seven hundred pounds of elk sausage, but as he modestly admitted, "The turkey was pure luck."

In northeastern Arizona, the neighboring towns of Concho and St. Johns tend toward differing citizenry. Many of Mexican descent and Roman Catholic faith reside at Concho and are known to take a drink; at St. Johns live many Mormons, who abstain. But the towns coexist peacefully, and neighbors even go hunting together. One cold morning in a duck blind on a windswept lake, the Catholic was warming his insides with gulps of whiskey. The Mormon drank warm milk from a Thermos. At last along flew a lone canvasback, and blam blam, the Mormon missed with both barrels. The hombre from concho stood shakily, and got the duck at eighty yards with one shot. Then he apologized, "Usually, I get four or five birds from a flock that big." Which brings up Giles Goswick's story about the three lyingest hunters from the town of Mayer. "I'm one," Giles would say, "and my boy, George, he is the other two." George claimed that as a wingshot, he always got one-for-one: "One dove for one box of shells."

Ed Echols, longtime Tucson constable and champion rodeo roper, bragged he found a gold nugget in the craw of a turkey, and his family ate nothing but turkey for a whole summer.

It was Ralph Watkins Junior who claimed the salt cedar thickets were so dense along the Gila River, his bird dog had to back up a foot or two in order to point. And Ben Vance's old Carolina hound was so eager, Ben had to put a patch over one eye to prevent the dog from chasing two rabbits at the same time. Not all dog stories end happily. Bob Boze Bell, the cartoonist, remembers a Mohave County beagle that was so-o-o-o smart, you could show that dog a tanning rack, and he would bring back a wild animal skin to fit it; one day, the mother got down the ironing board, and they haven't seen that beagle since. My own prize gun dog, a big, black cocker named Sugar, was considered powerful smart in a hunting camp. He would take his place in a circle of quail hunters, slip the celophane off a new deck of Bicycles, shuffle, ante, offer the cut, and deal a hand of draw.

"Aw, he ain't that bright," I'd tell the other players. "Whenever he holds three-of-a-kind or better, he wags his tail."

Sugar's more noble talents emerged in the field. Arizona quail tend to run rather than fly, so Ol' Shoog was trained to quickly circle a covey and drive the birds down a convenient gopher hole, which he then covered with a front paw. On signal, he would let the birds fly out, one at a time. That is, unless I called for him to release a double.

Jim (officially James E.) Cook quotes Jerry Clower about an old Arizona sodbuster who killed flying game birds with his ugly, ugly grin. One opening day of dove season west of Buckeye, envious hunters watched in awe, and commented, "Amazing. Do you know anybody else with such an ugly grin?"

"Yep. My wife."

"Well, why don't you bring her along to hunt?"

"Her grin is so ugly she tears up too much of the meat!"

When Judge J.W. Aker was living a quarter of a century ago, he liked to dress up like a dandy, trim his mustache, and honor any convenient saloon with his tall-tale repertoire. This much was truth: He had been justice of the peace, educator, newsman, soldier, miner, rancher, farmer, and political power broker of eastern Arizona. A Virginian, he had lost an arm and a leg in a Pennsylvania mining accident, and fled westward when well-meaning friends tried to make him into a charity case.

Likely truth was somewhat diluted when Judge Aker took his first sip of beer.

"Gentlemen," he would announce, "I have the largest cabin in Arizona. At one time I had twenty-one and one-half Akers under one roof. Since I lost a hand and foot, I only consider myself a half-Aker.

"Well, once when I was superintendent of schools I took a high school class to the mountains for an outing. Naturally, I packed a quart of whiskey for treatment of snake bite.

"After a week it looked like I never would get bit. One day I was fishing—had my attention on a tangled leader, and a kid shouted, 'Look out, Judge, you're about to step on a snake!'

"Sure enough, there was a big diamondback a-layin' on a rock. I put my wooden foot on top of it, so that about six inches of the head end of the rattler was free. The snake turned and struck my wooden ankle time and again.

"I shouted, 'Hurry up, you kids, run to camp and get a rope and that bottle of whiskey!'

"When they got back I had killed the snake with my fishing pole. The kids tied the rope in a tourniquet around my pants, and they handed me the bottle. I took all that I dared to take. The kids didn't catch on until they had me back to camp and tried to dress the wounds."

Sometimes Judge Aker would add a sequel. He said his wooden leg swelled up so bad, he was able to saw off enough lumber to frame his cabin and throw up a board fence around all twenty-one and one-half Akers.

Snakes can be goshawful bad medicine in the Sonoran Desert. One old prospector dispatched a rattler and tossed the dead critter into the fireplace of his cabin. The smoke from the poison blistered the logs, asphyxiated a pack of hounds, barbecued a burro, drove rats out of the neighboring cabins, killed the prospector, and persisted through three generations of buzzards. Possibly, however, that was an unusually frail prospector. Another story tells of an Arizona miner who was bitten by a rattler, and despite all medical treatments, the snake died anyway.

Animal husbandry reached a zenith at Northern Arizona University in Flagstaff. A professor who was also a fly fisherman developed a strain of cow that would stand patiently on the bank of a trout stream. The cow would switch flies, trout would leap to catch the flies, and with her tail, the cow would flip them onto the shore.

When Phoenix was just a little bitty frontier village, Sing High, proprietor of the most popular Chinese restaurant, supposedly was followed home by a desert mountain lion.

"Ah, so," said Sing on discovering the cougar's paw prints commingled with his own. "Honorable cat likes my tracks. So now, for him, I make more!"

I never did believe V.T. Henrick of Mesa. He said he went deer hunting on Upper Roosevelt Lake. He spotted a big buck and fired. The rifle blew up. The barrel sailed down Tonto Creek and killed five hundred ducks and the stock flew up the creek and killed five hundred geese, the bullet went straight ahead and killed the deer, the ramrod nailed a rattlesnake, the recoil knocked him into the lake, and when he swam ashore his boots were full of bluegills.

Needless to say, John Hance of Grand Canyon fame had a favorite fish story. He said it happened when a flash flood trapped him in a side canyon. All he had as a survival kit was a plug of tobacco. John said he picked up a mesquite club, tossed his chaw into the muddy Colorado, and poised at bankside.

Then he clobbered the fish when they came up to spit. Only trouble, "I was getting pretty tired of eating raw fish by the time the flood was over."

When I was producing a daily column for *The Arizona Republic*, it was my professional duty to tell the truth and nothing but the truth. Here's part of a piece I swore to one autumn:

It being that golden moment of the year for Arizona sportsmen—with the streams and lakes and mountains uncrowded, and seasons open on a variety of species—I dreamed up the perfect expedition. Three comrades went along, making a Jeepload, what with all the grub and gear.

We made the narrows of Saguaro Lake, where the lunker bass were striking every cast. Of course, I caught the most, counting the stringer of panfish and the biggest of the seven-pound-class largemouth. On the way we tarried over a muddy point and picked up a few catfish. Nothing real big, mostly around four pounds, but one old channel cat that fought so hard it worked up a sweat.

Then we drove up the Beeline to the Punkin Center turn-off and immediately encountered an enormous covey of Gambel's quail. The birds refused to run . . . in fact, huddled under little bushes until we kicked them up one at a time. My! Our shoulders got sore!

Down on the Tonto we strung out in the arrowweed and pretty soon flights of mallards and bluebills began to plummet into the eddys. Everybody got a limit. I was the only one to complain, "Doggone it, men, my freezer at home is already full of bandtail pigeon, turkey, and a quarter of last year's elk, plus thirty pounds of javelina sausage."

Anyway, we sashayed up to Rye for rabbit, and at a little old cattle tank no bigger than a mail-order swimming pool, we surprised a gaggle of geese. Mine were butter fat. So were the cottontail. The other hunters had to resort to shotguns, but I made do with my .22 pump. Before midafternoon, I had enough to fill my annual squirrel pie feast for five hundred guests. I know this is becoming unbelievable, but honest Injun, between Little Green Valley and the Diamond Rim Divide a full-grown tom cougar dashed under the wheels of the car. The fellows voted to give me the pelt, because I was driving.

We found Christopher Creek deserted. Although stocked rainbows were scarce, the larger German brown could be coaxed from their cut-bank haunts by adroit presentation of flies. My friends would have done better if they hadn't spent so much time studying my techniques. Soon as I had my limit, I lit out for Christopher Mountain. Parked the Jeep under a big old juniper and walked a loop through the oaks, where I figured a muley buck would snooze through the day—and sure enough, he jumped out going forty miles per in gigantic leaps, so that when the shot was perfectly placed, he landed, field dressed, in the back seat of the Jeep. On investigating a strange squawking, I found a hen turkey on the floorboards. The force of the fatal blow had knocked all her feathers off. Lucky for me, I had my turkey tag.

Back at the creek, my friends had resorted to corn, cheese, and doughballs in attempting to match my catch on flies. I was generously giving advice when lo and behold out of a patch of doghair pine charged an enormous black bear. I deftly fetched my book of game regulations and was pleased to note that after the first of September bear legally could be taken. But there seemed to be some question regarding the taking of more than one big game animal within any given calendar year, so I had to refer to the index for additional guidance. Just as the jaws of the brute closed on my throat, I woke. My old spaniel was licking my face, and the aroma drifting into the den from the kitchen definitely was from a bucket of the Colonel's chicken.

Bob Whitaker, now of some notoriety as a western outdoor writer, was born in Iowa. Bob harbors a grudge against folks who fish Iowa waters. They tell lies, such as, the fish are so big that when they outgrow a lake, they jump to a bigger one, and that is when they are vulnerable. Iowans use butterfly nets to catch them. Where a river is harnessed to a water wheel, the fish are too big to turn around between the banks, so they have to speed downstream, go around the mill wheel, and head back upstream. Bob wishes Iowans were more like Arizona fishermen, "who, when they catch a fish, have to blow the dust off to determine which species they've caught." Bob also says that bass are easy to identify. The small-mouth bass are males, and the large-mouth bass are females. So says Bob.

If Not the Tallest Tales, Certainly the Deepest

Even if he had not fought on one side or the other of the American Civil War, even if he hadn't been promoted or demoted at least to captain, even if he hadn't excelled as a freighter, trailblazer, prospector, host, and miner—John Hance's niche in southwestern history is secure.

Some tales during his times were told taller. Some shorter. But none were deeper than those invented and expanded by "Captain" Hance pertaining to Golly Gully, or more officially, Arizona's Grand Canyon of the Colorado River. The canyon is, by most estimates, the largest onshore hole in the world—or as Dr. Joseph Wood Krutch would more elegantly put it, "the most revealing single page of earth's history open on the face of the globe."

Yet that wasn't enough for Cap Hance. Author Gladwell Richardson knew Cap, and collected "Hance-y fancies," including the following:

I was mining where the canyon is now. Had ahold of a wheelbarrow and was coming out of the tunnel. I heard a whoop and a holler. Looked up and saw a thousand Indians right on my heels a-swinging their tomahawks at my hair.

That was no place for me. I couldn't turn loose the wheelbarrow. Them Indians was sure after me. By the time I outrun them, the Grand Canyon was dug and when I emptied the wheelbarrow, the San Francisco Peaks was built. By Dads! It sure was a horror but I managed to save this hair from them pesky Indians.

In other versions of this spellbinding adventure, Hance would allow the Indians a final victory. On a doleful note, Hance would tell his circle of tourists, "Them redskins killed me."

In truth, Cap Hance did not excavate the Grand Canyon. Nor did the WPA. Nor did the National Park Service. Nature labored ten million years or more to carve a chasm two hundred thirty miles long and eighteen miles wide through the Colorado Plateau. In 1540, Don Garcia Lopez de Cardenas was the first European leader to encounter the canyon, and, finding himself halted in his tracks, bitterly complained, "Those who stayed above had estimated that some huge rocks on the sides of the cliffs seemed to be about as tall as a man, but those who went down swore that when they reached there these rocks were bigger than the great tower of Seville." American James Ohio Pattie in 1825 summed up his reaction in one word: "Horrid." Army Lieutenant J.C. Ives reconnoitered the canyon in 1857 and reported to Washington, "Ours has been the first and will doubtless be the last party of whites to visit this profitless locality. . . ."

His error was obvious by the time Tennessean Cap Hance arrived in the 1880s. As the canyon's first permanent white resident, Hance witnessed an increasing procession of visitors. The early record of his life is clouded by his own outrageous contradictions, but quite clearly Hance joined with other pioneers in building trails and opening mineral prospects. Sapling-slender, blue of eye, tanned and wrinkled, Hance (subsidized by the Fred Harvey Company for tourist enjoyment) gradually emerged as the champion yarn spinner of the canyon country. Among more than a hundred deep tall tales attributed to Hance (Cap seldom repeated a story exactly or credited his own source) are the following:

Through Homer Wood comes John's near-disaster with a stranger, who asked him: "How's deer hunting around here?" Hance replied, "The best in the West! Why, just this morning I killed three bucks all by myself."

"Wonderful!" said the stranger. "Do you know who I am?"

"Nope."

"I'm the game ranger."

"Well, do you know who I am?" Hance went on.

"No."

"I'm the biggest damned liar in Arizona!"

Of his prowess as prevaricator, Cap once told a friend, Mrs. Elisabeth B. Heiser, "I've got to tell stories to them people...and if I don't...who will? I can make these tenderfeet believe that a frog eats boiled eggs; and that he carries the egg a mile to find a rock to crack it on."

Lon Garrison through the late 1940s gathered and set down Hance whoppers, this from Emery Kolb: Cap was forever boasting of his vegetable garden. One day a dude incautiously wondered how he watered the plants. Hance said, from the Colorado River. You carry the water up a mile? No, Hance confided. He said he had a strong pair of binoculars which he focused on the distant river and in the magnified image, "the water's only about six inches below the rim and I can siphon it."

Bob Wingfield, longtime storekeeper at Camp Verde, was especially bemused by Cap's explanations of his bachelor status. His eyes would brim with tears as he sobered a knot of sympathetic dudes with vivid descriptions of his wife one day falling over the canyon rim. "Broke her leg," John would say. "Had to shoot her." On other occasions, Hance confessed he once was married, but that he and his wife divorced. "We couldn't get along...so we divided what stuff we had. I kept the house and gave her the road."

According to one Godfrey Sykes, Hance had his fill of a young woman botanist in his tour. She was constantly plucking leaves and spouting Latin names as Cap waited his chance. "Wonderful organism, the tree," she told him. "Do you know it really breathes?" Hance responded with an air of grateful surprise. "That explains something that has puzzled me for a long time. I used to make camp under a big mesquite tree, and night after night that thing would keep me awake with its snoring."

Then there is the tale of the rubber-booted tenderfoot who tripped over the rim but remained upright. Off the canyon floor he bounded again and again, higher than the rim. "In the end," drawled John, "we had to shoot him to keep him from starving to death."

Another Wingfield, Charlie of Prescott, overheard Hance bragging to an Englishman on his gold pocket watch. Worth over two hundred dollars, said John. Sturdy, too. Why, once he dropped it, and it landed hundreds of feet below, on a little ledge. Yet after Hance spent three days climbing down to the watch, he found the timepiece unharmed, and running accurately. "Pretty good," Charlie thought, "for a twenty-four hour movement."

General Bulletin No. 6, July 1, 1942. Authority—Dr. D.T. McDougal. "It was a delicate job to know when the winter was actually beginning. Each season I timed my departure with reference to two things: the lowness of my grub supply and the near approach of a heavy snowfall. One night when I was all set to get out, a terrible storm came. It lasted two or three days. I contrived a pair of snowshoes and started from camp. After a few hours travel with these snowshoes...I fell and hurt my ankle so bad that I could not go any farther. However, I managed some way to work my way back to the cabin.... There was nothing but a jar of sorghum molasses and a box of Babbitt's Best Soap. I prepared a mixture of soap and molasses in a skillet, slicing the soap into flakes and adding a few shavings from an old boot leg to make the mixture as tasty as possible. Ladies and gentlemen, that was all I had to eat for a week...and I expect you to believe me, I have never liked the taste of soap from that day to this!"

At the Grand Canyon, where in the real world rainstorms actually mature below the rim, Hance wrung every drop of climatological fantasy. Hance said the canyon, once a lake, was formed during a cold spell when a flock of ducks, feet frozen in the ice, flew away in unison. Sometimes fog in the canyon got so thick, Cap could walk across on snowshoes. One time when the fog unexpectedly dissipated, he was marooned for a month on Zoraster Temple. He escaped on a much lighter fog—"But I was much lighter by that time, too." Hance might conclude this marvel by offering to lend his snowshoes to the nearest tourist.

Lockwood credits Edgar Whipple with saving some of Hance's bigger-than-life bear adventures. By ever-edited causes, a particular bruin was goaded into a rage that it vented on poor Cap Hance. "Every minute I thought he'd get me by the Levi's. I sighted a big pine ahead with a limb about thirty feet up.... So I made a big jump for that limb—the biggest jump I ever made in my life. I missed it entirely! That is, I missed it going up, but I caught it coming down."

Homer Wood once told Lon Garrison, "If Baron Munchhausen and John Hance had been alive at the same time, the Baron would have been John's secretary." Offered in evidence, "One time John saw a fox chasing a rabbit....After several hours, both animals were so tired that they lay down to rest. By a curious coincidence, both were females and each gave birth to young during the rest period. When they recovered, they started on, with the mother fox chasing the mother rabbit and four little foxes chasing little rabbits.

Common fibs that the Colorado during flood off Bright Angel Point was too thick to drink and too thin to plow were beneath (pardon pun) Cap Hance. Dr. McDougal recalled John's narrow escape when kneeling to quaff his thirst at riverside. The mud was, well...thick! "I tried to bite it off, but my teeth were too poor for that. Finally, I managed to pull my hunting knife out of my boot and cut off the water."

White Mountain Smith was witness when a dude approached Hance for directions to the river.
"Right down there." (Pointing down a vertical mile.)
"Does it ever flood?"
"Yes, it does. Gets pretty high, too."
"How high?"
"See that point over there," John explained. "Many's the time I've ridden over there, got off, and watered the horse right from the canyon rim."

A frequent ally in Hance's miracles was his horse, Darby. (Or sometimes, Roany.) Darby was the one killed in an attempted leap across the canyon. Hance survived by yelling whoa at the last moment. Simple enough, Hance had only three feet to fall, but poor Darby had to fall three thousand. But when Hance discerned that he had an audience of tourists hypnotized, he would swear, straight-faced, "We were both killed."

Of course, not all thigh-twacking utterances inspired by the canyon can be traced to Cap Hance. Stuffy old French Field Marshal Ferdinand Foch gazed from his mule into the abyss and mused, "What a marvelous place to throw your mother-in-law." Mounting a canyon mule, Soviet cosmonaut Georgy Beregovoy gravely announced, "If I perish, I left my will in my hotel room." The mules, then, deserve some credit for seven decades of inspiration, while packing tens of thousands of skittish dudes down Bright Angel Trail to Phantom Ranch.

According to John Bradley, mule skinners are often asked for a gentle mount. The standard reply: "Sorry, we just let the last gentle mule go with the last bunch. We'll give you a brand new one and you can both learn together!"

It helps not at all when the laconic trailboss adds, "Don't you worry none. I ain't never lost a customer yet. . . . 'Course, this is only my first trip."

John Hance died at about eighty years of age on January 6, 1919, and was buried almost within sight of the South Rim near the Shrine of Ages Chapel. Edna Evans, who measured between his headstone and footstone, states the distance is precisely twelve and one-half feet. His bronze tablet memorializes his career as guide and trailmaker, but perhaps his epitaph and eulogy were better written by gullible admirers of another generation.

In Cap Hance's guest book on October 1, 1898, R. and E.E.P. Skeel scribed:

Farewell to the gorge
And to Captain John Hance.
Whose mendacious inventions can outdo all romance.
With his fibs he can charm you, with his yarns
    he enchants.
And as if these great gifts to still further
    enhance—
With a bolster he is going to learn how to dance.
Oh, may we return—by some rare, happy chance—
To this spot, and be welcomed by Captain John Hance.

Before the turn of the century also, was composed this salute by Hamlin Garland:

The man who ought to be remembered with the Grand Canyon of the Colorado is not a scientist, nor a painter, nor a poet. He is only an old pioneer who has summered and wintered with the Grand Canyon for twelve years. His name is John Hance. . . .

Your friends who have been to the canyon will say: 'See the canyon, of course, but don't fail to see old John Hance,' and I hereby celebrate, also, the personality of the man who made this canyon his home when it was practically an unexplored wonder. . . .

There are those who laugh at John Hance and see nothing in him. Others acknowledge him to be a powerful and astonishing fictionist. Consciously, he is a teller of whopping lies. Unconsciously, he is one of the most dramatic and picturesque natural raconteurs I have ever met. . . . His gift for telling phrases is as great in its way as that of James Whitcomb Riley. His profanity is never commonplace. It blazes out like some unusual fireworks and illumines his story for yards around. It is not profanity; it is dramatic fervor. . . .

He does not fear to be out of the world for he has beside him one incontestable wonder of God's Earth. If he waits long enough, all the world will come to him. All the poets and all the scientists and geologists—all the people really worth knowing will come to see old John and his canyon, and I hereby say deliberately they are both worthwhile.

He Put in His Hip Pocket a Damn Good Cow Ranch

The southwesterner who drifted naturally into telling the tallest of tall tales was the cowman (if an owner) or cowboy (if a hired hand). Daily range-riding duties routinely required heroic physical activity. The country loomed gigantic. And the risks of rearing savory beef in the raw wilderness never abated. Life in all aspects was an outrageous gamble—so why not also recreation?

A 1900 editorial in the *Phoenix Enterprise* observed: "A wide open town is Phoenix at present. Gambling halls are cheered by girls and liquor is sold in the same room, thus embracing the three great evils under one big tent. It is not difficult to answer the question, 'Where is your boy tonight?'"

Pioneers engaged in games of chance as an early sport, perhaps the first, in the land we now call Arizona. All of the town of Show Low changed ownership in the turn of a card. That is not a tall tale, but the truth.

The May 9, 1887, issue of the *Coconino Sun* detailed an encounter between two giant sportsmen of the early Arizona outdoors. They were Captain B.B. Bullwinkle and Frank Vanderlip, neighboring cattlemen who played poker in a humble log cabin on the outskirts of Flagstaff. That neither had much money posed no obstacle. Said Bullwinkle, "I propose we play one-steer ante, two steers to open, no limit." Vanderlip agreed.

The Captain dealt and Vanderlip anted one steer. Both came in and the game opened with four steers on the table. The Captain drew two tens and caught an unexpected full house, while Vanderlip dropped out.

The next hand was a jackpot and it took three deals to open it. Vanderlip finally drew two jacks and opened the pot with a fine breeding bull, which counted for six steers. The Captain covered this with five steers and a two-year-old heifer and went him twelve better.

Vanderlip saw the twelve. Each player drew three cards. Vanderlip caught a jack. Then...went him fifty steers, twenty two-year-old heifer calves better. The Captain looked at his hand and placed upon the table sixty-five cows, five bulls, one hundred two-year-olds, fifty prime to medium steers, with a side bet of a horse and a saddle to cover the bar bill.

Vanderlip made his bet good with an even two hundred fifty straight half breeds and twenty-four mustangs and the Northwest quarter of the Southwest quarter of Section 10 Township Range 2 East, and called.

The Captain held three aces and got up and put in his hip pocket seven hundred sixty-two steers, bulls, and heifers and a damn good cow ranch with a large herd of mustangs.

The game, incidentally, was not the end of Vanderlip. He soon recovered his losses and went on to become the president of the Chase National Bank in New York. Cowboys nowadays would say that Vanderlip's luck ran a little muddy, that his pockets sprang a leak, and that "if he didn't have bad luck, he wouldn't have no luck a-tall." But not to worry. Before long Vanderlip had "more money than he could keep dry."

Far from town, beyond the reach of newsboys and before the invention of electronic communications, cowboys had to rely on their own resources for humor. Laconic, convoluted, conspiratorial jokery grew out of the fertile soil of American folklore and flowered in forms peculiar to a lifeway manifestly lonesome, dangerous, introspective, outdoor, workworn, shy, unintellectual, and male. "To understand ranch lingo," Philip Ashton Rollins quoted a cowboy, "all yuh have to do is to know in advance what the other feller means an' then pay no attention to what he says." Although the joke endures, the value system embraced by such types is all but gone. Ramon F. Adams: "Unlike us, to him money meant nothing. He would work hard for thirty dollars a month, then spend it all with his characteristic freeheartedness in an hour of relaxation. All he was seriously concerned about was plenty to eat, a good horse to ride, a saddle for his throne, and he was King."

In such a world, overstatement became understatement, and vice versa. And the nearest topic for discussion was the ever-present horse. Johnny Bixler, an old rancher in the Bill Williams country, used to brag about a pony: "He's only got two little faults. He's hard to catch, and not worth a damn when caught." Doc Bill McGrath (although a psychiatrist, not a cowboy) had heard of a cow pony with three gaits: "stumble, falter, and fall." Ben Perkins, another Bill Williams cowman, claimed a horse so touchy to ride, he didn't dare shift his chaw of tobacco from one cheek to the other. When Frank Honsik wasn't bragging about his buckskin, Golden Nugget, he said other people's horses were so sorry "they'd buck the whiskers off a man." Val Stannard said the toughest horse she ever rode was a "hammerhead that had eaten a breakfast of bedsprings," named R.I.P.

Boasting in the tradition of Davey Crockett followed the sun itself westward. When asked about his home town, a Texas cowboy would tell his Arizona bunkmates, "I'm a bad man from Bitter Creek. The farther up the creek you live, the badder you get, and I lived in a camp beyond the last house."

As Charlie Pickrell told it, his best friend, Manford Cartwright, rode in off the range to attend one of the early Arizona Cattle Growers conventions in Tucson. That city had just installed electric lights, which were new to Cartwright. The bellboy failed to tell him how to turn out the light. Pickrell: "When bedtime came, he wanted the light out. After several failures in attempting to blow it out, he thought of a plan—he tied one of his boots over the light and accomplished thoroughly satisfactory results."

They were lucky to get Cartwright into the hotel at all. Another old cow waddy of that era was asked what hotel he was staying at in town. He replied, "Hotel? Why, I'm only gonna be in town four days!"

Port Parker of the Verde Valley dealt in the stuff of legends. A friend accused him of spreading the word around Sedona that he was a son of a bitch, and Port pleaded innocent, saying, "I never said you were a son of a bitch, and I don't know how folks found out."

It was Port who watched in awe as bulldozers converted an old horse pasture into Robert Trent Jones's Oak Creek Country Club. "M'gawd," said Port. "I spent a lifetime clearing and flattening that land...and now you've gone and put all the hazards back."

When John McCarroll was printing one of the West's liveliest newspapers at Wickenburg, he told about two cowboys who received horses as presents.

They had trouble telling the horses apart. One brother cut off his horse's mane. This worked...until the mane grew back. The other brother cut off his horse's tail, but in time that grew back, too. Finally one of the brothers got a bright idea—they'd measure their horses. And by golly the white one was a good three inches taller than the black one.

Cowboys are notorious for their poor memories of names, and maybe it was McCarroll who snitched on Frank Allen, retired rodeo cowboy and head wrangler at Wickenburg's Rancho de los Caballeros.

"Frank," his boss told him one day, "we've got a very important guest. You remember his name! It's Colonel Armstrong."

The wrangler memorized the name. He repeated it aloud as he did his chores. "Colonel ARMstrong. Colonel Arm-STRONG. Colonel ARMSTRONG!"

Next day Colonel Armstrong appeared at the corrals. "Howdy," shouted Frank, rushing up with extended hand. "I'm Colonel Armstrong."

The first half of a cowboy's professional name drew a fair share of comment. Pioneer Tonto Basin rancher George Cline feigned amazement every time a cow tried to outrun a roundup: "Them damn fool cattle think they can outrun us—with us horseback and them afoot."

Needless to say, such intolerable conditions justified strong medicine. Legendary is the cowboy who worried about the quality of his whiskey and sent a sample to the assay office for analysis. Back came the report, "Sir, your horse has diabetes." The result of such poison: "My mouth tastes like I've been eating with the coyotes." One bar served a complimentary snake with every shot of Old Squareface, causing customers to wonder aloud how the distiller managed to keep the stuff corked. Many's the mythical cowhand who turned down a raise because his liver could not survive another ten dollars a month. But for every one like that, there was a cowboy who would go into a saloon, look at a drunk passed out on the floor, and say to the bartender, "Pour me the same, and make it a double." He may have been the one-of-a-kind cowpoke who bragged he came from a family of long livers: "Why, grandpa had a liver thi-i-i-s long!"

Marguerite Noble again: "Dick Robbins, oldtime rodeo hand, was holed up in a hotel room with some fellow contestants. The boys were celebrating with liquid refreshments. . . . This particular evening one ol' boy, quite likkered up, declared he could jump out of the window and fly around the building. The bets were on. The performer staggered to the open window, waved his arms toward the heavens—and jumped. Landing in the bushes below sobered him. Wobbling dazed back into the room, he attacked his partner's loyalty with, 'Why'd you let me do that?' His partner hiccuped and explained, 'I thought you could do it. I lost ten dollars on you.'"

Dude eastern women frequently play a role in cowboy humor. Ignorance of the ways of western livestock provides a familiar theme. As Tempe's Charlie Pickrell used to explain to the Connecticut lady, "Yes, I'm hitching this prize bull to the plow. For two years he has been tearing down fences to get to my neighbor's cows. And today I am going to teach the sonofagun there is more to farming than romance." According to Tom Power, a Back-East lady stepped off a Greyhound bus and asked him which side of a cow he was fixing to brand.

Tom drawled, "Why, the outside, ma'am."

63

Nor was any male dude so important or powerful to buck the unwritten rules of the range. Bona fide cow country author Marguerite Noble wrote in *Arizona Highways* magazine:

> The cowboy was a self-styled aristocrat and individualist, unlettered and impoverished as he might be, taking guff from no man. In 1918 Zane Grey and entourage camped in an isolated craggy section of central Arizona where supplies were packed in long tedious miles by horseback. A cowboy, needing work, agreed to do the cooking. Two horsemen came by, and the cook invited them to "git down, coffee's ready." Later Grey informed the cook that this was HIS camp and feeding passersby was not permitted. The cowboy told Grey, "When I'm doin' the cookin', any feller what comes by is invited to grub." Stillness held the camp in abeyance. The ponderosa pines stopped bowing; the blue jays ceased complaining; and the gray squirrels retreated to the high branches. The author backed down. The cowboy cook remained and reigned.

Generally scarce in cowboy land, womenfolk attracted a variety of treatments. According to Marguerite Noble, a cowboy might say of a shapely schoolmarm, "She's built like a quarter horse on a Tijuana track"; of a woman past her prime, "Long in the tooth." Children might be called "yearling"; a woman, "an ornery old heifer"; a comely maiden, "a young filly"; a slender young horsewoman, "she could sit a saddle on a fifty-cent piece and show money from all angles," and thus endowed, "had a short rope but could toss a big loop."

A well-behaved lady was "scarier'n bein' left afoot." A man pursuing a serious romance with a respectable woman was especially vulnerable. During one Frontier Days doin's at Prescott, a cowboy joined the festive parade down Whiskey Row with his best girlfriend riding at his side. On signal, all the upper-story windows of Prescott's sporting houses flew open, and the soiled doves yelled at the cowboy, "Hello, honey!"

Oren Arnold delighted in documenting the method two cowboy bachelors devised to hasten the departure of two plain dude female cousins, both given to meddling. The ladies offered to wash dishes after the first evening's supper, but one of the cowboys said, "Never mind," and whistled in a brace of hound dogs, who licked the plates clean before they were stacked neatly in the cupboards. The ladies left the following morning. The cowboys then boiled the dishes and lived happily ever afterward.

Another of Charlie Pickrell's heroes was Tot Young.

> While I was county agent of Yavapai County, a girl in the East wrote me saying she would like to correspond with a real cowboy. Tot Young was still a bachelor, and since I knew Tot to be a real old cowhand, I gave her Tot's name. Soon after, Tot received a letter.
>
> So Tot dutifully took up the job of writing letters to the eastern lady. Soon she asked him for his photograph. Tot replied, "I don't think postal regulations would permit my sending such material through the mail, but I'll try to give you a description of myself. I'm supposed to be one of the homeliest men in Yavapai, and that is one of the largest counties in the United States; the barber can cut my hair with my hat on; and I know I have a good set of teeth because I paid sixty-five dollars for them less than two years ago."
>
> The next time I saw Tot, he said, "You know, I never heard any more from that girl."

Without doubt the most eloquent cowboy Arizona ever produced was Henry Fountain Ashurst, who was one of the state's first United States senators. He said he rode the range with a miniature *Shakespeare's Works* in the hip pocket of his jeans. Ashurst confided that he learned to speak against the northern Arizona wind, and claimed that he could "toss a fifty-two-pound word all the way across the Grand Canyon." One Sunday, his trail outfit ran plumb out of food and coffee only a day's ride from Winslow, where, on the Santa Fe mainline, flourished a fancy Harvey House: gourmet meals, silverware, beautiful waitresses. There was no stopping the horse race; Ashurst could only go along to avert trouble. The gang of grimy, gamy trailriders was halted at the dining room door by a stuffy maitre d' who decreed: "Gentlemen, coats are required."

Sensing big trouble, Ashurst held a pow wow with his men and devised a strategy. They all donned their rain slickers, which reeked of water-repellant fish oil, and reappeared on the dining room doorstep, with Ashurst the spokesman, "Sir...we are wearing our coats!" In the truce that ensued, the cowboys were served a sumptuous meal by the Harvey Girls, in the restaurant kitchen, free of charge.

Among the witty, honest, poetic, salty, and wise utterances of Ashurt later in Washington are the following:

On deeds: "Good words are the sons of Earth. But good deeds are the daughters of Heaven."

On success: "The welfare of the United States, and the happiness of our people, does not hang on the presence of Henry Fountain Ashurst in the Senate. When that realization first came to me I was overwhelmed by the horror of it. But now it is a source of infinite comfort."

On failure: "No man is fit to be Senator . . . unless he is willing at any time to surrender his political life for a great principle."

On mixed drinks: "I've killed a lot of hostesses' rubber plants by pouring cocktails into them, and I don't drink that much. Notice how I mix it. I pour the whiskey carefully, and it stays on top. I'm drinking whiskey, just slightly cooled by ice and water. You've got to have a drinking program."

On youth: "Youth should be prudent along with its boldness—for youth has much to lose; therefore, do not sow your wild oats in youth; you might live to reap the terrible harvest. Sow your wild oats in your old age and you will not live till Harvest Time."

On friends: "I have no trouble with my enemies, but my friends, they're the ones who keep me walking the floor nights."

On death: "There either is or there isn't a hereafter. If there is, I'll be there. If there isn't, I'll never know. But if there is an eternity, I don't think God will say, 'Henry Fountain . . . you've cavorted and raised hell and broken my Commandments . . . so you'll have to stay out.' No, I don't think He'd want to run a Heaven that would keep Henry Fountain Ashurst out."

I Can't See the Train...
It's Forty Minutes Late

The state with more national parks and monuments than any other can scarcely be accused of exaggeration. Consequently, not all of that which follows can be certified as the untruth, and nothing but the untruth. Reality in wide open spaces of the far Southwest has a way of authenticating the unreal.

Take Petrified Forest National Park (on second thought, do not...pilferage of even a tiny bit of petrified wood is against the law). Scientists want us to believe:

What today constitutes the world's greatest exposure of petrified wood began as living plants some two hundred million years ago. In that primordial world, ferns loomed as large as trees, and bus-size reptiles lumbered through the swampy gardens where perhaps the first flower bloomed.

Layers of earth a half-mile thick were eroded from this place: bit by bit, mountain by mountain, removed by a drop of water, a wedge of ice, a puff of wind.

Maybe dinosaurs were warm blooded. And feathered. And colored shocking pink. Nobody can say no.

Does the pronuba moth think? It has struck a partnership with the fineleaf yucca. The yucca will not make seeds unless the moth fertilizes the flower. The moth cannot incubate eggs unless the yucca produces seeds. So the moth without apparent reward carries pollen to the plant's stigma. Does the yucca think?

A thousand years before the discovery of the New World, now-vanished peoples converted the vast expanses of what is now the national park into an open-air, astronomical observatory. The evidence remains, clearly chiseled into the rock.

So with all of that, the truth, what chance, a mere fib? But we must try.

At Flagstaff, the Santa Fe agent will say, "There's a train due in here in forty minutes. But I can't see it, so it must be running late." One old Arizona mountaineer rose every morning at 5 a.m. He had no radio, telephone, clock, or rooster. Puzzled neighbors hid out one night to learn his secret. Just before retiring, he lifted his bedroom window, and bellowed, "Wake up, you dang old fool!" The voice took all night to bounce off the farthest mountain, and arrived back home just in time for reveille.

Distances in the Land of the Long Eyes can be misleading. Buck Saunders insists that not far from a Wickenburg guest ranch a dude had taken off all his clothes and was about to dive headfirst into the Hassayampa River's tiny rivulet. A passing cowboy asked why, and the dude replied:

"Yesterday I tried to hike to those mountains, only to discover they are twenty miles away. Now I want to cross this wide, wide river, and I'll not be fooled again!"

Bernie Maher used to guide tourists at Monument Valley, a holy place to the Indians deep in Navajoland, and setting for some of the classic western movies. Ernie would gather a circle of tourists, wave a hand at the thousand-foot-high sandstone mittens and say, "Why, I've been guiding in these parts since these monuments were only three feet tall...." Bernie also took credit for the exquisite, virgin ripples imparting such intriguing composition into color photographs. Every night after all the tourists, sheep, and Navajo herders retired, Bernie would sneak out to the dunes with his rake and restore the ripples.

Life in the wide open spaces stimulates an independent spirit.

Once, a city motorist screeched to a halt in front of a Chino Valley house where cords of cedar bore the sign, WOOD FOR SALE. The stranger asked, "Do you take orders for firewood?" The Chino woodchopper sitting on the porch slowly set the record straight: "I do have wood. Sometimes I sell it. But, mister, I don't take orders from nobody!" When U.S. Route 66 connected little bits of nowhere with long stretches of nothing, a sign on a Winona service station stated: "We sell no gas on Sunday. And damned little on weekdays."

Times have changed (it's hoped) since speculators with little sensitivity toward nature divided large tracts of Arizona into "ranchettes" without roads, water, or power. Gone are the days when advertised "electricity on property" meant no more than the high voltage lines from Davis Dam to the big city. But in jest, Ted Day confides that he has put all of his money into property at Somerton, south of Yuma on the California line. "I figure there's enough sand down there to make a wonderful beach when the earthquakes cause California to break off and sink," says Ted. When the fever was highest for land speculation some years ago, the story went around that a developer rushed into Phoenix and told his partner, "We can get title to a hundred thousand acres for only a million dollars! But there's one hitch...we've got to put five hundred dollars down...."

Now, choice parcels of Arizona land sell for a million dollars an acre. No joke. Five acres sold at that price in Scottsdale in 1985. Quite a contrast from the report of an Arizona visitor in 1861:

With millions of acres of the finest arable lands, not a single farm was under cultivation in the territory; with the richest gold and silver mines, paper money is the common currency; with forts innumerable, there is scarcely any protection of life and property; with extensive pastures, there is little or no stock; with the finest natural roads, traveling is beset with difficulties; with rivers through every valley, a stranger may die of thirst. Hay is cut with a hoe, and wood with a spade or mattock. In January one enjoys the luxury of a bath as under a tropical sun, and sleeps under double blankets at night. There are towns without inhabitants and deserts extensively populated; vegetation where there is not soil and soil where there is not vegetation. Snow is seen where it is never seen to fall and ice forms where it never snows. There are Indians

71

the most docile in North America, yet travelers are murdered daily by Indians the most barbarous on earth. Mines without miners, and forts without soldiers are common. Politicians without policy, traders without trade, storekeepers without stores, teamsters without teams, and all without means, form the mass of the white population.

Fred Eldean, known to deal in hundred-thousand-acre parcels, still shakes his head over a report from Omar Gould, Pine stonemason. Two hunters from the big city were considered lost when Omar encountered them crossing State Route 87 from one dense forest to another north of Strawberry. "Why didn't you boys follow the road?" Omar asked. One replied, "We didn't know where it went."

Arizona abounds in the most curious, most spirited, most evocative place names in the world. There. The brag is made. Let the burden of disproof rest with residents where there are no towns named Bumble Bee, no creeks named Quien Sabe, no hills named Squaw Tit, no municipal memories named Copperopolis. Let them belittle the verve of Mrs. Ninon Talbot, when she moved from Los Angeles to the Arizona desert, where she claimed to be the "biggest real estate operator in the business, and at three hundred pounds, maybe she was." She set out to found a town on the windy, waterless, scrubby flats west of Kingman, and she named it Santa Claus. For years, folks from all over the world shipped their Christmas cards to Mrs. Talbot for that frosty cancellation.

Where thrives a more unusual name than Show Low? Two Arizona pioneers dissolved their partnership in a card game called Seven-up. With their townsite as stakes, Marion Clark announced, "If you can show low, you win." Corydon Cooley said, "Show low it is," and the turn of his card won—and named—a town.

What a place for a namedropper...in Arizona...fifty or a hundred years ago. Many places already had names, of course. Native names. Many are still around. But Europeans in ethnocentric compulsion renamed them—indelicate (until recent decades a range near Yuma went by Shithouse Mountains), descriptive (there's only one Camelback), imaginative (an Apache County boulder covered with petroglyphs, Newspaper Rock), editorial (there's Sockdolager Rapid and Hardscrabble Mesa), ominous (beware of Bloody Basin!), biological (guess what infested Lousy Gulch), provocative (where else, the Lost Dutchman Gold Mine, but deep within the Superstition Mountains?).

Mysteries abound. The origin of the name for the farm community of Eloy between Phoenix and Tucson seems utterly lost. And although songwriter Bobby Troup in his hit song, "Route 66," cautioned, "don't forget Winona," eventually the interstate bypassed Winona and for love, chalk, or marbles, the source of the name is forgotten.

Yet the process of name-giving goes on. Miracle Valley. Leisure World. The border inspection station changed from Gripe, Arizona, to Smile, Arizona. Peggy and Jim Kater in 1949 settled at the uninhabited junction of Arizona highways 85 and 86 down toward the Mexican border, where one wilderness larger than some New England states has not one permanent resident. At first, the Katers had no water well, no electricity, no telephone. The nearest name was "The Y," referring to the road forking off to Ajo on the west, Tucson to the east, and Mexico to the south. Slowly, the conveniences of the twentieth century arrived, along with a few residents. The Katers founded a general store, which eventually attracted a post office.

When the postal service asked for a town name, Mrs. Kater submitted "Why," along with a touching explanation, "Why do we stay in Why? We love the beautiful sunsets, the clear, smog-free air, the giant cactus, the first cool breeze from the gulf on a hot summer's night, and most of all our good neighbors and friends. Why name it Why? Why not!" And that is why Why is.

On the subject of placenames, no Arizona author contrived a more sensuous statement than the late Ernest (Foxtail Johnson) Douglas. His verse is repeated here with the permission of another cherished friend, Toni Nelson:

Belle of Bumble Bee

I have roamed from Patagonia to Fredonia,
    And many loves in many towns I've had.
I just can't forget Rosita whom I wooed in Sahuarita,
    Nor Beula, my beloved in Bagdad.
I have sweethearts in Canoa, Quijotoa,
    Cibola, Chaparral, and Cherokee.
But of all the girls I've flattered there were
    none who really mattered
    Save bonny, beaming Belle of Bumble Bee.

There's a peach in Adamana, name of Anna
    And Susie sighs for me at Cedar Glade.
At a place called Palo Verde is a charmer
    known as Birdie.
    In Agua Fria dwells my Adelaide.
I have soul mates in Kayenta, Caliente;
    In Nutrioso Nettie waits for me.
But there never was a cutie like my bouncing
    blue-eyed beauty,
    My buxom, blooming Belle of Bumble Bee.
There's a dear in Arizola, name of Lola
    And Angela calls me to Paradise.
By the border at Nogales sits my tricky
    tipsy Alice;
    Kathleen of Cottonwood is mighty nice.
I have flames in Coconino and Querino,
    Tollchaco, Tapco, Tombstone, and Tempe,
But there never was a lassie who was half
    so sweet and classy
    As bashful, blushing Belle of Bumble Bee.
There's a maid at Hotevilla, name of Prilla,
    And Pearl expects me back at Pomerene.
I had quite a case on Berta, who resided
    at Ligurta;
    Luisa loved me madly at Laveen.
I have lost my heart to Pozo and Plomoso,
    Carrizo, Calabasas, and Chin Lee.
But no fractious female flung me down
    so hard, or ever stung me
As did the blondined Belle of Bumble Bee.

On the subject of size. Often Hendrik Van Loon is credited with a humbling image: that if all the people on earth could be tucked into one box, it could be hidden out of sight in one minor side tributary of the Grand Canyon. Consider that a portion of Arizona about the size of Manhattan (roughly twenty-five thousand acres) would not be enough ground to support a very small cattle ranch in the Southwest. On a June crosscountry cavalcade by the Coronado Trail Riders, the thirty horsemen ascended Eagle Creek, tarried for lunch at Honeymoon Cabin, climbed up to Luna Lookout, took a detour through Bear Wallow, slept in a dry camp above Black River, and settled in on Reservation Creek—a distance of a good hundred miles—and saw exactly one stranger, an Apache cowboy putting out salt for tribal cattle. One early October morning recently, a man and his wife drove southward nearly ninety-five miles along U.S. Route 666 (the Coronado Trail) and passed one lonely Jeep. New York's Central Park at eight hundred forty acres is a little bitty lawn. The world's champ municipal park is Phoenix's South Mountain: 16,169 acres. Of Arizona's nearly seventy-three million acres, only seventeen percent is privately owned. Arizona claims creation's largest unbroken stand of ponderosa pine—two hundred fifty miles long. Residents of Moccasin try to keep their government visits to a minimum; it's a three-hundred-fifty-mile drive—one way—to the county seat of Kingman. That pointer, properly called a gnomon, in the center of the village of Carefree north of Phoenix makes that sundial the largest in the Western Hemisphere. And southward to Tombstone, the eight-thousand-square-foot Lady Banksia is said to be the largest rose bush on earth.

They Had to Shoot a Man to Start the Payson Graveyard

lsewhere, the weather can turn terrible. And admittedly, in other regions, abide climates that permit the continuation of life. But in and around Arizona, the serious boast is made that no other region in the nation enjoys so much meteorological variety so beneficial to human health.

Blue northers in Texas come on so fast they've been known to overtake a sweating, galloping horse at the barn door and flash freeze its hindquarters. Wind gauges in Colorado commonly consist of an anvil hanging from a logging chain (when the chain assumes a horizontal attitude, it's considered the first indication of a zephyr). In Montana, summer may last an entire day, which often corresponds with the closing and opening of ski season in Idaho. One year it got so chilly in Oklahoma a politician was observed on a street corner with his hands in his own pockets. Impressive cold snap, that. An early Nebraska newspaper reports a tornado that "turned a well inside out, a cellar upside down, moved a township line, blew all the staves out of a whiskey barrel and left the bunghole, changed the day of the week, blew a mortgage off a farm, blew all the cracks out of a fence, and knocked the wind out of a Populist!"

But these manifestations pale when compared to Arizona's

Grand Canyon, where in reality summer may blaze at the bottom while frost nips the rims. Or to Tucson, where an hour's drive in climatological terms may equal a drive from semitropical Mexico to subarctic Canada.

As a point in fact, not all the wind at Winslow was generated by J. Morris Richards when he was publisher of *The Winslow Mail*. With Richards as our witness, that high, treeless plateau country does seem to attract bodacious blows. At peak gusts, according to Richards, it takes four men and a small boy to nail a cowhide over a keyhole.

Once on U.S. Route 66, a windblown lass protecting her modesty with both hands screeched at a Winslow resident, "Does it blow this way all the time?" The reply: "Only half the year. The other half a year it turns around and blows the other way."

Actually, life would scarcely persist in all the Four Corners country (where the borders of four states intersect) if it weren't for the weather holes. These are deeply drilled into bedrock. Lengths of drill steel are cemented into the holes. When the wind reaches enough velocity to bend these steel shafts to a forty-five degree angle, citizens shoo the children inside. When the rods are blown horizontal, the womenfolk head for the house. And when the rods shear right off, the men follow.

Only in January may there be a brief respite, when the weather holes are repaired. From Gray Mountain Trading Post on U.S. Route 89 to Navajo Bridge, there descends a vast envelope of dense fog. The moist air hangs for a week or more, keeping temperatures day and night around freezing. According to James F. Collins of Page, the pea soup plays havoc with communications. Jim says icicles trap telephone talk. Once, Jim's office telephoned Phoenix requesting information too confidential to send by radio. But the call did not go through. Jim's engineers calculated the location of the freezeup. A Navajo line scout was dispatched to the thirty-third telephone pole beyond the Little Colorado bridge, and broke off the seventh icicle south of that pole. The Indian took the icicle into the warm cafe at Cameron. He held a tape recorder next to the ice and captured the conversation as it thawed.

Then the message was relayed into Phoenix from Gray Mountain. The Phoenix office responded, but as before vital instruction was frozen into the line. Before the icicle could be located, a California family stopped to admire the visibility of one hundred yards. A small boy tossed a rock and dislodged the conversation-enriched ice. And then, Jim swears, as the boy licked the icicle, complicated engineering formulas seemed to float from his mouth. Too bad, the California family sped away so fast they didn't see the weather holes get back into operation.

Then Arizona cold. Julius Festner attests that out on Mingus Mountain the falling mercury pulled all the fasteners out of the thermometer. They got around that in Williams by fitting the mercury with a rubber bulb. That was the day in Flagstaff that a dog running across the Museum of Northern Arizona parking lot froze stiff with all four feet off the ground. So cold it set George Babbitt's teeth to chattering—and they were in a water glass in the bathroom. The very air froze; two girls in Seligman engaged in an argument, which piled up as ice cubes, to be used later to cool the Gatorade for the debate team.

Boosters of the Arizona desert climate concede to other areas the prize for snowfall, but as one desert rat observed, "One hundred ten degrees in the shade may be a little uncomfortable, but at least you don't have to shovel it off the driveway." So sunny and balmy are the days, Casa Grande has ceased judging women by their clothing. Insufficient evidence.

Arizona rainbows frequently occur as triplets, but do not lead to pots of gold. Instead, at the end of an Arizona rainbow repose detailed directions to a good Mexican-food cafe. More precious than gold.

It happens, too, that the Mogollon Rim lying athwart Arizona's middle, ranks among the more thunderstruck features on earth (you could look it up). One stupendous bolt hit the exhaust stack of a Northern Arizona fossil fuel power plant and reversed the generator, which then caused the turbine to run backwards and produce a thousand tons of coal.

What the Arizona desert may lack in snow it more than makes up for in flash floods. Not funny, unwary motorists on sunkissed roads have been overtaken by the runoff from storms many miles distant. "Caution, Dip Ahead," is a sign encountered on secondary roads, and the first rule of low country camping is, "Never throw down your bedroll in a dry wash." A family of backpackers from New Jersey ignored a little cloud twenty miles away and no bigger than a man's hand, and they were swept away to join a Princess Cruise to Acapulco.

Arizona sunsets have precipitated international incidents. The

Russian newspaper *Pravda* more than once has accused *Arizona Highways* magazine of brightening photographs (the magazine is officially banned in the Soviet Union). But over the years editors steadfastly refute the charge—on the contrary, the photography is dimmed to save the eyesight of readers!

Tornadoes touch down infrequently in the far Southwest, but the local twister, the dust devil, fills the void. These circular winds draw power from sun-induced thermals, and the summer day is rare that a horizon is not dotted with devils sucking dirt, litter, and freshly washed clothes hundreds and even thousands of feet into the sky. Generally brief in duration, a few persist. One dust devil ground away in the same spot for three days before a Gila woodpecker drilled a hole in it and broke the suction.

Astonishing weather. But healthy. When Fred Eldean was eighty-six he was still working out daily at a Scottsdale fitness center where the other customers—all older—tipped him handsomely to carry in their barbells. The only people who die in Scottsdale are cemetery-lot brokers, of starvation.

Our late and lamented Charlie Pickrell had an anecdote illustrating the healthfulness of Arizona air. He was a student at the University of Arizona when he received a telegram: YOUR MOTHER HOSPITAL LOS ANGELES STOP RECOVERY NOT EXPECTED STOP COME IMMEDIATELY. Charlie's only means of transportation—in fact, his only possession—was his bicycle. So he pedaled to L.A. and for safekeeping, he carried the bike to his mother's intensive care ward.

"Unbeknownst to me," Charlie asserted, "a bullhead sticker was in the front tire, and the tube chose that moment to blow out, filling Mom's room with clean, healthy Tucson air. She miraculously recovered so completely, I was able to bring her home on the bike!"

Nobody ever gets sick in Payson. They had to shoot a man to start the graveyard there, and then they had to hide his head in the mausoleum so he couldn't find it. Jim Young, active in the Chamber of Commerce, attributes his own splendid health to the Payson climate. He and Dorothy, when they were married more than thirty years ago, struck an agreement—when she was angry, she would go to the kitchen, and Jim would wait on the porch. "To that I attribute my longevity," said Jim. "A healthy, outdoor life." Four doctors in Payson went broke for lack of medical practice, but one got rich growing fishing worms.

Among supportable Texas brags is a trend to windiness (most generated in-state). One Michael Grant, himself a tad windy but a splendid writer, took his West Texas heritage westward to San Diego and preached in the land of fruits and nuts. He told Californians about wind. The Beaufort Scale, so familiar to dwellers of the Pacific coast, was useless on the Texas plains, said Michael. Texans developed their own chart, listed below in condensed form.

> *Force One*, breath of air. Not much wind, yet.
>
> *Force Two*, breeze stirring. Open newspaper; if disappears, breeze stirring.
>
> *Force Three*, good breeze. Cannot button coat; wash on line dries before you can return to house.
>
> *Force Four*, little wind. Red wall approaching on horizon represents top inch of Oklahoma, Kansas, and Dakota soil. If cloud turns green, likely tornado. Schoolkids still play at recess.
>
> *Force Five*, windy. Neckerchief worn in hip Levi's pocket will flap you to death.
>
> *Force Six*, blowing up a gale. Domestic animals flying by your window not wearing your brand.
>
> *Force Seven*, blue norther. Cars and trucks flying by have Canadian plates. Texans always comment, "Boy howdy nothing 'tween here and the North Pole but a bob war fence."
>
> *Force Eight*, solons' wind. Named for Texas state legislature. "The kind of wind that engineers worry about when designing tall buildings.

Mike is not sure that he ever experienced a solons' wind, although as a sports writer he witnessed some terrifying effects—the look on a quarter-miler's face when he made the first turn into a Force Six, and the anguish on the face of an Amarillo baseball infielder who threw a ball into the first base dugout. "Why the hell didn't you throw to third base?" screamed the manager. The infielder said, "I did."

But according to resident veterans of the Four Corners, those Texas gusts are puny puffs on the high mesas of Colorado, New Mexico, Utah, and Arizona. They've heard about the Nebraska hen that in a high wind laid the same egg five times. But in Ashfork they have to mix buckshot in the hen scratch to keep them from blowing away. The power poles are on hinges, so they can be raised easily after every storm. One day, the wind across Lake Mead shoved all the reflected scenery onto the eastern shores, and delayed sundown three hours. All the barbs in all the wire fences of the Hualapai tribe were blown down to the corners. A Mexican woman was flattened so flat against a flat cliff she couldn't eat anything but flat tortillas for ten days flat. A three-thousand-foot-deep helium well was blown out of the ground and an enterprising Indian cut it up into six-inch sections to sell as balloons at the Navajo Tribal Fair. Fortunately, the well was rescued by joining a thousand yard-long fence post holes blown in from Farmington. The wind blew away all the headstones from the Kingman cemetery and returned the next day for the manhole covers.

But after all the huffing is done, Winslow's the windiest. Some years ago when *The Arizona Republic* ran a tall tale contest, this was the winner:

Winslow's winds are legendary. Trees grow sideways. Flagpoles are tripods. Stopped trains have the wheels chocked. Buildings have angled walls to offset the force of the wind. It's said the Tower of Pisa was built by a contractor who lived here too long.

The residents have adapted well. They lean at a forty-five degree angle when walking. They don't have a dentist clean their teeth—they just smile during a sandstorm and the tartar is blasted right off.

Newcomers sometimes have problems. Shortly after his arrival, a Chamber of Commerce manager held a kite-flying festival. Several participants had to be hospitalized for rope burns. Next he organized a "Predict the Highest Wind" contest for television weather forecasters. None of the entries was within the required fifty miles per hour, and all had to be disqualified. Then he became enthusiastic about windmills as a source of energy, but they went over the maximum RPM and the bearings burned out. . . .

The airport has special problems. One pilot neglected to use full throttle during landing and was blown backwards off the runway. Another complained he used more fuel taxiing to the terminal than he did flying from Seattle. . . .

Helicopter pilots who stop overnight at Winslow airport are cautioned to remove their rotor. One pilot used a log chain to secure the rotor . . . and the next morning he discovered his aircraft hovering at five hundred feet with the rotor merrily freewheeling. Two cowboys practicing team roping finally lassoed the 'copter and brought it down.

The highway patrol warns drivers of trailers and campers about the dangers of high winds. But no one thought to notify the railroad and a train with ninety-seven empty cars was blown over. . . . If you decide to investigate all this yourself, you can't miss Winslow on Interstate-40. As you leave the town, you'll see signs reading:

CAUTION: CALM AIR

Of Dog Tails Alligorpions, and Sand Trout

A timeless moral echoes from history in the tragicomic tale of the Guzzling Bear of Brewery Gulch.

The true story dates to the boomtown years of Bisbee, Arizona, before the turn of the century when Main Street boasted its own stock exchange, and its side street, Brewery Gulch, had twenty-five saloons. Main Street was for banking business, but as Frank Brophy explained, Brewery Gulch was for monkey business.

One day, a miner brought to the Gulch a bear cub captured in the Huachuca Mountains. Joe Muheim, proprietor of the Brewery Saloon, accepted the bear as a gift—a novelty that might attract some customers. This, br'er bruin did, almost too well. In those times of hardrock drilling, Bisbee was populated by Cousin Jacks, Polacks, Chaws, Bohunks, Swedes, Mexicans, Indians, and a few blacks; they all worked hard in the mines, and played even harder in the Gulch. In such a robust gathering, a bear seemed the ideal plaything.

First the men cultivated in the bear a taste for beer. Soon, that bear could chug-a-lug a quart of lager faster than the thirstiest timbersetter. Yet the bear's ability to hold his liquor proved no greater than human. Four or five steins and the bear was bombed. A crooked grin distorted his furry face as he lurched down the bar to mooch another glass from an obliging miner.

Then some unthinking powder man taught the bear to box and wrestle. Naturally inclined, the bear would return smack for smack, hug for hug. There's no record that the bear ever resorted to tooth or claw, but plenty of times, a miner who challenged the bear was slammed the full length of the Brewery bar, which measured a good fifty feet. When the bear was an adolescent, the fights usually ended in a draw. But the beast matured as aggressor, and never lost.

The monster began to worry Joe Muheim. Inevitably, he knew, somebody would be crippled or killed. Muheim's worst fears almost came true one day when a small girl accompanied her father into the Brewery. While the gent chatted with the barkeeps, the half-stoned bear ambled over to beg for a piece of candy. The girl hid her candy sack behind her back. A mistake. The intoxicated bear then seized the child, and would not release its grip until Muheim scattered the candy on the floor.

The bear had to go. But how? Before Muheim could act, fate intervened. Customarily, the bear was chained to a large cotton-wood tree next to the Brewery at night. No matter how drunk, the bear would stagger up the trunk and pass out in a notch of limbs. On a morning soon after the incident with the girl, the bear was discovered dead, hanged by his chain.

It fell to William Epler, modern-day editor of *The Brewery Gulch Gazette*, to articulate a lesson from these happenings. Bill's moral: "If you get drunk, don't sleep in a tree. But if you do, make sure you don't have a chain around your neck."

How can a tall tale top a true story like that? Retired navy commander Ray Duus used to grieve over a fancy tropical fish he brought back from duty in the South Pacific. Arizona posed an environmental challenge. First Ray weaned the fish onto fresh water, and gradually onto the dry air of the city of Mesa.

"Got to where it would follow me about the yard and even down the street. But tragedy struck. We got caught in a line squall. Having lost its former sure-finnedness, it slipped into the gutter and drowned."

Kathy Dean won a tall-tale contest perpetrated by Sam Lowe of *The Phoenix Gazette*. Went like so:

The Phoenix iceman delivered from a horse-drawn wagon in the old days. The merchant roamed the streets, yelling, "Ice! Ice! Ice!" One day a pedestrian walked near the horse and thought he heard it mumble. "Did you say something?" the pedestrian asked. "Yes, I said I'm really tired," replied the horse, who then launched into a tirade about how his new owner worked him twelve hours a day on weekdays, sold rides on his back to kids in the park on Saturdays, and rented him out to church groups on Sunday. "Well," said the pedestrian, "if it's so bad, why don't you tell him you can talk?" And the horse said, "Never! He'd have me yelling, Ice! Ice! Ice!"

If you ever begin to feel important, goes an old adage, try bossing somebody else's dog around. Writers down through history took note of dogs. Shakespeare compared humankind to the dog world; students still wonder, when Lady Macbeth cried, "Out damned spot!" why she wanted the dog to leave. Mark Twain stated, "If you pick up a starving dog and make him prosperous, he will not bite you. This is the principal difference between a man and a dog." Josh Billings added, "Money will buy a pretty good dog, but it won't buy the wag of his tail." Ambrose Bierce's *Devil's Dictionary* definition of a dog reads: "A kind of additional or subsidiary Deity designed to catch the overflow and surplus of the world's worship. This Divine Being in some of his smaller and silkier incarnations takes, in the affection of Woman, the place to which there is no human aspirant. The Dog is a survival—an anachronism. He toils not, neither does he spin, yet Solomon in all his glory never lay upon a door-mat all day long, sun-soaked and fly-fed and fat, while his master worked for the means wherewith to purchase an idle wag of the Solomic tail, seasoned with a look of tolerant recognition."

That's an insult. My Ol' Shoog more than made up for my poor skills with a shotgun. Out in the grain fields west of Buckeye, he would fetch limits of doves downed by other hunters. But my dog was never as keen as a pair of hounds known to Charlie Pickrell. At cattle roundup, one dog would throw and hold a calf, and the other would apply the brand and chew the ear mark. Once Charlie accused the dogs of misbranding a dogie, and they fetched the mother cow to prove they were right. But finally, the dogs lost their job.

They got to where they insisted on doing the roping while Charlie did the branding.

Mickey Whiting would never tell ba-a-a-d jokes about shepherds not seeing the ewe turn. But he does entertain at formal state dinners with the following:

> Seems an El Paso ventriloquist received a summons to perform at Las Vegas. Halfway across Arizona in the remote sheep country, his van broke down. Only a lone herder with his flock, his horse, and his dog were in sight.
>
> "'Preciate some help with my van," said the showman. But the sheepherder refused, saying, "Oh, no, I could not abandon my responsibility to my flock, not for one minute, no, sir."
>
> So the ventriloquist threw his voice into the dog, which seemed to say, "This man is terrible. He beats me and starves me." Then the ventriloquist threw his voice into the horse, which seemed to say, "This man is a brute. He never grooms me, and he forgets to let me drink." Then the ventriloquist turned to talk to a nearby ewe. But the sheepherder interrupted, insisting, "Ah, my friend, let us go fix your van!"

Those who know a bit of Arizona history reject the term, "man-made," for most public works. They were "mule-made." The broad, deep main canals, the excavations for dams to bedrock, the cuts and fills for the first highways, the leveled fields—all were mostly accomplished with the power of mule muscle. "Much has been written about the Spanish horse in the conquest of the New World," Professor Max Moorhead has stated, "but the unsung hero of transportation in the Southwest was unquestionably the Spanish mule."

The opinion is seconded by Floyd E. Ewing Jr.: "In fact, between 1820 and 1860, the role the mule played in the great task of subduing virgin lands and fashioning channels of trade and commerce in the Southwest was just as spectacular and just as important as that of the mustang or longhorn." For the roughest sections of his stagecoach route, John Butterfield preferred mules. To suffer defeat at Little Big Horn, Custer rode a horse. To capture Geronimo, George Crook rode a mule. Crook's lieutenant, John G. Bourke: "The mule will go ninety miles for you in a day and night without water, but he sees no sense in wheeling around and doing fours right and left and back and forth and over and over again on a parade ground. . . . So he quits. . . . Don't think a mule lacks courage, though. He stands fire better than most horses, all recruits, and many a western soldier."

The hybrid offspring of a jackass and a female horse, the sterile mule seemed particulary responsive to verbal abuse. Charlie Niehuis tells of an early day muleskinner who out of respect for a preacher passenger, attempted to drive a team with clean language. After a while the parson said, "Whyant you cuss 'em out, Jake. Let 'em know what you want 'em to do. You're goin' to Hell anyway if you keep drivin' mules."

By registered mail came the testy memo from the honorable Jack Williams, reigning Governor of Arizona, and the world's second-worst fisherman. "You are the duly appointed official Arizona State Jackalope Inspector, and you are late with your report," he chided.

And his excellency was correct. The paperwork had indeed fallen behind, with the jacklope commission spending most of the year in the field so as to confirm that sightings of the creature were in direct ratio to the distance from Arizona saloons. Now prodded by the chief administrator, the commission labored past midnight to complete the following report:

1. To date, in all the state's history, there has been no authenticated capture of a native jackalope, alleged to be a cross between the jackrabbit and the antelope. A horned hare, if you will, and you will. Many authorities, including some sobersided game department biologists, doubt that the jackalope exists in Arizona's wilds.

2. Yet sightings persist, strangely enough, most commonly after dark by citizens homeward bound. The most compelling evidence: the increasing numbers of stuffed jackalope heads displayed behind the bars of the state's saloons. Thus, where the species abounds, the commission devotes its efforts.

3. Also supportive of jackalope existence: numerous other hybrid

creatures flourish. Alligorpions are bred with alligator heads and scorpion tails by zanjeros to keep small children out of irrigation canals. Chuckamonsters and gilawallas sun themselves on the red hot rails of the Arizona Western Railway at Quartzsite. So why not rackjabbits?

4. Our plan to find and crown a Miss International Jackalope Queen has infuriated certain political movements. Some of us commissioners were interviewing a bevy of willing candidates at the Five O'Clock Lounge when a woman customer stubbed out her cigar, knocked back a jigger of rye, and used a strange term. As if we did not have our hands full with the queen contest, now we have to determine the definition of a male chauvinist pig.

5. We're getting nowhere with the Boone & Crockett Society toward establishment of standards for measuring jackalope heads. The Big Ten hunters snub our efforts to expand the list to The Big Eleven. Your own Department of Fish & Game not only refuses to set seasons and bag limits, no action is taken against poachers.

6. The Arizona Legislature hasn't provided the commission with an enforcement arm. Thus, the display (and sale!) of counterfeit jackalope heads snowballs to a consumer-fraud scandal. One phony trophy imported from Hong Kong was found to be covered with human hair. Sonoran child laborers are weaving inferior jackalope heads from goat hair.

7. That slot machine disguised as a stuffed jackalope still hums along in the Bisbee Elks Club. You put a quarter in its ear, haul down on the left horn, wait for the eyeballs to stop spinning, and get the payoff through the nose. If the state will provide per diem, the commission will check out the Elks. There's supposed to be a couple of chauvinist pigs there, too.

8. We're putting in for a Defenders of Wildlife grant. Propagating jackalopes makes about as much sense as restocking grizzly bears and timber wolves.

9. The commission has a Draft Environmental Impact Statement in the works. Deja vu. Trouble is, we can't agree whether the study should be the impact of man on the jackalope, or vice versa. The lady at the Five O'Clock wanted us to make it the impact of man on woman, which is outside the commission's official purview.

10. In line with federal guidelines, the commission is perfecting a comprehensive jackalope fee system . . . say one dollar to camp near a jackalope, two dollars to photograph a jackalope, and ten dollars to eat a polish sausage or pickled egg in a jackalope-improved saloon. In a program inspired by the United States Forest Service, we propose to pay a jackalope ranger eighteen thousand dollars a year to collect eight thousand dollars in fees. Double both figures if it's on Indian recreation land. Triple the figures under the jurisdiction of the Bureau of Land Management.

Respectfully submitted, by your commissioners:

The thirty-six-year-term, Hunter McWilliams of Bowie, the only man known to have made a pot of chili out of jackalope, WOB (without beans).

The thirty-year-term, Joe Billingsley of Cameron, first with the theory that silicone pebbles, heretofore considered of volcanic origin, actually are petrified jackalope pellets.

The twenty-four-year-term, Dick Waters of Kingman and Baja New River, who once, while fishing Lake Mohave for crappie, cast so far up the bank he hooked a jackalope, thereby saving you, Mr. Governor, the title of world's worst fisherman.

The eighteen-year-term, Norman B. Conkle of Florence, who probably has seen more jackalope than any living Arizonan.

The twelve-year-term, Bob Robles of Yumaphoenix, author of an unpublished, definitive, bilingual history of the Mexican jackalope, or anteconejolope.

The six-year-term, Jack Walters of Ramsey, whose bar may shelter the largest known coin-operated jackalope.

The two-year-term, George Ruiz of Clifton, gearing up for transcontinental shipments of commercially raised jackalope sub sandwiches to Karl Eller's Circle K Convenience Markets. (George's term is about to expire, which is just as well, inasmuch as the other day we caught him devouring a taco of jackalope, tomato, onions, cheese, olives, chili with beans, avocado, sour cream, and chives. The other commissioners doubt his loyalty.)

No Arizona humorist has emerged to rival the late Dick Wick Hall. (Disclaimer: excluded are postures of certain state senators of outrageously comical pomposity and omnipotence, but unfortunately for the democracy these affectations are not intended to be funny. One wonders what Hall today might manage with such fat targets.)

Mark Twain made the world think, then laugh. Will Rogers made the world laugh, then think. Had he lived longer, would Hall have gained his own greater rank as a wit? The man certainly chose a medium of small promise: a mimeographed, single-sheet sometimes-newspaper for one of the lesser populated regions of his time. Yet the world literally beat a path to his door.

Hall's town was Salome. He invented it. And he named it for a beautiful, demure tourist who took off her shoes to rest a spell, but "when her bare little feet touched the warm sands of the Arizona desert, Salome hotfooted her way to fame." In the first decades of motoring, Hall established a gasoline station in western Arizona. Down a dusty, dangerous track steamed the multitudes that would make the twentieth-century American movement the greatest migration in human history. Nearly all of Hall's customers were heading for California. Individually, the migrants often were ill, poor, weary, frightened, and grouchy. For Hall, despondency presented a vacuum to be filled with whimsy. "Smile, smile, smile," his roadside billboard read. "You don't have to stay here, but we do."

The pumps at his station dispensed Laughing Gas. Hall said he kept a frog that carried a canteen to moisten the moss on its back. "None of the natives ever die here," Hall would boast while wiping windshields. "At least, they never admit it." Hall spoofed golf, prohibition, women's makeup, county government, the Democratic Party, rich people, Boston, religion, and himself. In Hall's day, *The Saturday Evening Post* spellbound the nation. And in a success story typically American, the editors of the *Post* in the 1920s began to reprint the *Salome Sun* as a regular weekly feature, and a hundred newspapers picked up the syndicated column. Hall's mailbag acquired foreign postage. Fans wondered about his meandering, oddly capitalized style. He explained he had to type on a machine "with some teeth missing," and:

I think it Looks Better to have a few Capitals scattered around and break the monotony of so many Little Letters. I would use all Capital Letters if I thought it would make Folks Feel any Better.

To Hall, golf was a game of beknickered snobs. So he created the imaginary Greasewood Golf Course, laid out in rods instead of yards. Thus, Par 72 meant "seventy-two Days Going Around." A typical paragraph in the *Sun* reported:

J. Parker Bronsville of N.Y. was in Town yesterday and says he was chased by a Mountain Lion on the east side of Apache Peak out on the Greasewood Golf Course Wednesday afternoon. Indian Jack was sent out this morning to remove this Hazard and players will be allowed to Detour Temporarily and go around Apache Peak in going from the 13th to the 14th Holes, during which time the Committee has Ruled that Par for this Hole will be Two and a Half Days instead of the Five Days like it has been going over the Peak.

Every Hall addict acquired a favorite topic; revisited today, Hall's running commentary on women reminds us how long a way "baby" had to come:

Two women in One Town is Just a nough, or else several hundred. When there is only Two, all they can do is Talk to Each Other and Try to Listen, while they are thinking What they are going to say to themselves as soon as they Get a Chance; but when you get three, there is the Devil to Pay. Two can't say anything about Each Other except to Themselves and they have to be Careful, but when you get Three Women in One Town, they will all get to Twoing it back and forth and Talking about the Other One, no Matter which One it is. . . .

Hall also stage-directed a wildly original zoo in the theater of his mind. Of Gila monsters, "They are harmless, unless they bite you." Of animal husbandry, "Almost everything grows well here. Squint Eye Johnson built a barn last year and on account of the high price of lumber cut four big cottonwood posts and set them in the ground for the corners, nailing boards on to complete the barn. It rained soon after and the corner posts started to grow—and it kept Squint Eye busy all summer nailing on more board at the bottom to keep the cows from getting out—and now he has a two-story barn and uses the top story for a hen house. Squint Eye says one more wet year and he will have to buy an aeroplane to feed his chickens." Then, of politically burdened rabbits, "We are going to have a Jack Rabbit Drive next week and try to get rid of some of these Road Destroyers which keep running back and forth Across the Road until the Tourists can't tell which is the County Road leading to Los Angeles & the Promised Land. If we could ever get these Jack Rabbits Trained so as they would all run One Way and follow the same Trail, we would soon have a Better Road than the Supervisors ever built." But Hall's most complex creation was his "frog seven years old that never learned to Swim":

A Lot of Folks Wonder and Keep Writing me whether My Frog is All Bull or Just Some Frog and Some Bull, but I'm still claiming he's the Champion Seven Year Old Frog that weighs 27 and a Half Pounds and Whipped a Dog last year and is sure Some Bull Frog Both Ways from the Belt, even if he does live out here in this Little Colorado Corner of Hell and can't Swim. He don't like Cold Weather and He Sleeps all Winter in under the Floor of the Laughing Gas Station and don't Come Out until it commences to Warm Up a little, about 115 or 20 in the Shade, if there was Any Shade.

DeForest Hall, native of Creston, Iowa, and literary father of a dehydrated frog, died April 26, 1926, of a kidney ailment. He is buried in Salome. If Hall's career perished too early, that of the late Evans Coleman never got much of a start. Yet as his voluminous papers deposited at the Arizona Historical Society attest, Coleman pursued an old-fashioned literary style that was bulldozed aside by wisecracking comedians and televised trivia. Coleman told odd-creature stories that were not only tall, but LONG.

His convoluted windy about a powerful team of oxen requires about an hour to read aloud. The genuine turn-of-the-century Arizona cowhand and veteran bullslinger gratuitously includes spitting magic, animal psychotherapy, and male tribal rites. Eventually his ox team wins, but with such a monstrous tug they pop into a treetop. Coleman appears to be the originator of the antinugtallian, "a carniferous furbearer with legs short on one side for running hills south of Springerville." The varmint had a saving grace: preferred mothers-in-law for breakfast.

Now, Big Jim Griffith, resident folklorist on the University of Arizona faculty, would discern worthwhile social energy within the tales of range riders such as Coleman and the late Van Holyoak of Clay Springs. How a greenhorn might react to a gentle ragging might signal his reaction in a real emergency. And says Doctor Jim, "in a multi-ethnic, multi-skilled society, we need all the communication skills we can muster. Then, I can't shake the belief that stories are beautiful, and that human-made beauty is enormously important in any form. It is the only God-like aspect of the human condition. Tensions can be eased through the exchange of entertaining stories; we can get to know others better, and ultimately, feel better about ourselves." He says he is much encouraged by flourishing folklore: "The art of deceiving the outsider is very much alive and well in Arizona. There are still people who tell stories with the honest intent of seeing how far they can string their listeners along. Of course, there is a precedent for this in the Bible where it says, 'I was a stranger and you took me in.'"

Which is about as serious as Dr. Griffith bends, before relating the life history of the sand trout of the Santa Cruz.

We have tremendous sport fishing along our rivers, especially the Santa Cruz. The sand trout has evolved as the desert has dried out, and he's grown lungs instead of gills and his eyes are on long stalks so he can look for something to eat as he swims on the edges of the sand.

But he's a cagey fish—he sees so well—and fishermen have learned to be cagey to catch him. Some use hooks imbedded in prickly pear or cholla, but I think the best way to catch him is to catch him with a horned toad.

You tie a leader around a horned toad's belly and let him walk down right near the fish. He's got to get real close to the fish because the fish can't walk too far or he'll burn his scales on the desert sand. The horned toad has spikes on the back of his head, so once you've hooked a sand trout you can just reel him in. But if you're real hungry, you can haul him in hand over hand and he'll be cooked and skinned by the time you grab him.

It is true that horned toads are protected by federal law, but there's no law says you can't take them for a walk along the river.

At times, Big Jim is overtaken by a seizure of honesty, in which case he confesses that several years ago the Santa Cruz flooded, and all the sand trout perished.

Big Jim's counterpart at Arizona State University, Don L.F. Nilsen, whose paper, "Linguistic Humor in Western Literature," contends that there is a speciality about the language of exaggeration in the West.

Mody Boatright tells us that in the West something huge is a lalapalooza, something great is peacherino, and something heavy is poniferous. . . . Something that is not on a North-South-East-West plane is antigodlin or catawampus, and this could make a person discombobbulated. A simple word like very becomes all-fired in Western talk, as in "She's all-fired sweet." If something disappears suddenly it is said to have absquatulated, and a lively person is said to be rambunctious, or perhaps even all-fired rambunctious. . . .

And so on. A modern favorite of Don's is Arizona's comedy queen of Paradise Valley, Erma Bombeck. In *The Grass is Always Greener over the Septic Tank*, Erma tells of a latter-day suburban sandlot baseball game:

"This is first base," said Coach Corlis, dropping his car seat cushion on the ground, "and this is second," he continued, dropping his jacket, "and I see there's a third base." "But . . . it's a pile of dung," said one of the players. "So don't slide," said Ralph.

Of first rank among Arizona folklorists was the late Ernie Douglas, farm writer who adopted two of the West's worst weeds for his pen name, Foxtail Johnson. By the time he finished sixty years of writing, Foxtail had done about all that he could with simple snakes: so mean they'd steal lunch buckets from children; ordinary bears, so fierce if captured they'd help with the plowing; mere spiders, with a hundred legs and a bite on each one.

96

No. Ernie bred wonders. The augerino adept in letting water out of irrigation ditches. The alligorpion to scare kids away from canal banks (alligator plus scorpion). Ernie reported a hybrid of mule and dachshund: "Result is a very long mule which can easily carry twelve passengers at a time, single file, down the Canyon trails...." As far as research tells, Ernie hatched the tall tale of Nugget Doves all by himself:

> The Nugget Dove...would take nothing into its gizzard, in the food grinding machinery, but gold nuggets. There are also minor differences of plumage that could be detected only by experts, of which I am the only one extant.
>
> I was unaware of the existence of this strange member of the dove family until several years ago when I went prospecting in the Tedro Mountains. I didn't have much of a grubstake and soon I was reduced to mesquite beans and what game I could shoot, which was mainly doves. To my great delight, I began to find nuggets in the gizzards of some of the birds I prepared in my frying pan.

In short, Ernie discovered Nugget Doves, captured some, chummed them with grain, trained them to retrieve, and went to town with thirty thousand dollars.

> It was there I met a stranger and lost my gold. I only have myself to blame that I am not a rich man today. It was a very reckless wager I made with that stranger. I bet him I could tell a bigger lie than he could. But I never was any good at telling lies.

Selected Readings

Adams, Ramon F. *Cowboy Lingo*. Boston: Houghton Mifflin, 1956.

Arnold, Oren. *Arizona Brags*. Phoenix: The Bargeo Press, 1947.

_____. *The Wild West Joke Book*. New York: Frederick Fell, Inc., 1956.

Barker, S. Omar. *Legends and Tales of the Old West*. Garden City, New York: Doubleday, 1962.

Becker, May Lamberton. *Golden Tales of the Southwest*. New York: Dodd, Mead & Company, 1939.

Boatright, Mody C. *Folk Laughter on the American Frontier*. New York: Macmillan, 1949.

Botkin, B.A. *A Treasury of American Folklore*. New York: Crown, 1944.

Chittick, V.L.O., ed. *Ring-Tailed Roarers: Tall Tales of the American Frontier*. Caldwell, Idaho: Caxton Printers, Ltd., 1941.

Cohen, Hennig, and William G. Dillingham. *Humor of the Old Southwest*. Boston: Houghton Mifflin, 1964.

Davidson, Levette J., and Forrester Blake. *Rocky Mountain Tales.* Norman: University of Oklahoma Press, 1970.

Douglas, Ernie. *The Snake Stood Straight Up.* Tempe: Arizona Historical Foundation, unpublished.

Evans, Edna. *Tales from the Grand Canyon, Some True, Some Tall.* Flagstaff: Northland Press, 1985.

Gorman, Michael. *The Real Book of American Tall Tales.* Garden City, New York: Country Life Press, 1952.

Greenway, John. *Folklore of the Great West.* Palo Alto, California: American West Publishing Company, 1969.

Hoig, Stan. *The Humor of the American Cowboy.* Lincoln: University of Nebraska Press, 1958.

Meine, Franklin J., ed. *The Crockett Almanacs.* Chicago: Caxton Club, 1955.

_____, ed. *Tall Tales from the Southwest: An Anthology of Southern and Southwestern Humor.* New York: Alfred A. Knopf, 1930.

Nutt, Frances Dorothy, ed. *Dick Wick Hall: Stories from the Salome Sun by Arizona's Most Famous Humorist.* Flagstaff: Northland Press, 1968.

Rollins, Philip Ashton. *The Cowboy; His Characteristics, His Equipment, and His Part in the Development of the West.* Reprint. New York: Charles Scribner's Sons, 1936.

Schwartz, Alvin. *Whoppers.* Philadelphia and New York: J.B. Lippincott, 1975.

Thorp, Howard N. (Jack). *Pardner of the Wind.* Caldwell, Idaho: Caxton Printers, Ltd., 1945.

Tolbert, Frank X. *A Bowl of Red.* Garden City, New York: Doubleday, 1966.

Trimble, Marshall. *In Old Arizona.* Phoenix: Golden West, 1985.

Welsch, Roger. *Shingling the Fog and Other Plains Lies.* Lincoln: University of Nebraska Press, 1972.